Contents

Short guide to the European Convention on Human Rights

(3rd edition)

Donna Gomien

Senior Lecturer in Human Rights
Institute of Social Studies
The Hague
The Netherlands

Council of Europe Publishing

French version:

Vade-mecum de la Convention européenne des Droits de l'Homme (3ᵉ édition)

ISBN 92-871-5747-2

Cover design: Graphic Design Workshop, Council of Europe
Layout: Desktop Publishing Unit, Council of Europe

Edited by Council of Europe Publishing
http://book.coe.int

Council of Europe Publishing
F-67075 Strasbourg Cedex

ISBN 92-871-5670-0
First edition 1991, Second edition 1998
Reprinted with corrections January 2000
© Council of Europe, 1991, 1998, May 2005
Printed at the Council of Europe

User's guide

This *Short guide to the European Convention on Human Rights* is intended to provide a concise overview of:

- the case-law arising under the European Convention on Human Rights;
- the procedures followed by the European Court of Human Rights when reviewing individual petitions under the Convention; and
- the role of the Committee of Ministers as a supervisory organ, as well as that of the Secretary General of the Council of Europe in giving force to the European Convention of Human Rights.

As the title indicates, the Guide is intended to be *short*. The chapters on the substantive rights guaranteed by the Convention address only some of the most important and/or most current judgments of the Court. They do not discuss many of the interesting, but more peripheral cases, nor do they discuss unsuccessful claims and the reasons for their failure, although such a review would also be instructive. The Guide covers the case-law under the Convention to the end of 2003.

The sections on practical procedures focus mainly on applications from individuals, not states. In the interests of space, the Guide uses the terms "Convention" and "Court" to refer to the European Convention on Human Rights and European Court of Human Rights. The terms "Convention institutions" or "Convention organs" refer to the (now defunct) European Commission of Human Rights and the European Court of Human Rights taken together. On the few occasions when the Guide refers to applications, it refers to them by their numbers only.

In the interests of readability, full titles and details of the cases do not appear every time a case is mentioned. In its discussion of the case-law, the Guide uses the following citation forms to mean the following types of decisions and judgments:

Appl. No. or application: refers to an admissibility decision of the European Commission of Human Rights or the European Court of Human Rights;

(date): refers to the year of a judgment of the European Court of Human Rights.

Also in the interests of readability, the terms High Contracting Party, Contracting State, State Party and State will be used interchangeably throughout the Guide.

Although both the French and the English versions of the Convention are considered to be authentic, the Guide does not address the differences in language between the two versions. I have used the English version when writing this Guide.

This *Short guide to the European Convention on Human Rights* intentionally limits its scope principally to the case-law and procedures of the European Court of Human Rights. Owing to the lack of space, it does not address many other matters of interest for those engaged in regional or international human rights law. It does not mention the European Social Charter, for instance, which governs the protection of economic and social rights within many Council of Europe member States, the European Convention for the Prevention of Torture and Inhuman or Degrading Treatment or Punishment, or the two regional instruments addressing the rights of minorities; nor does it address itself to the various human rights initiatives of the political bodies of the Council of Europe or those of the Organization for Security and Co-operation in Europe (Human Dimension) or the role of the European Union in protecting certain human rights. Likewise, it does not discuss the extensive human rights machinery of the United Nations and its specialised agencies.

Introduction

1. The Statute of the Council of Europe

From the very genesis of the Council of Europe, the principle of respect for human rights has been one of the cornerstones of the Organisation. At a meeting in The Hague in 1948, the Congress of Europe acted as the catalyst for the creation of the Council of Europe, adopting a resolution which reads in part as follows:

> The Congress
>
> Considers that the resultant union or federation should be open to all European nations democratically governed and which undertake to respect a Charter of Human Rights;
>
> Resolves that a Commission should be set up to undertake immediately the double task of drafting such a Charter and of laying down standards to which a State must conform if it is to deserve the name of democracy.

The main substance of the first of these two propositions was included in the Statute of the Council of Europe as Article 3:

> Every Member of the Council of Europe must accept the principles of the rule of law and of the enjoyment by all persons within its jurisdiction of human rights and fundamental freedoms....

The importance of human rights is emphasised in several other provisions of the Statute of the Council of Europe, and Article 8 even provides that serious violations of human rights and fundamental freedoms are grounds for suspending or expelling a member State from the Council.

The Statute was signed on 5 May 1949. The drafting of a human rights charter was a high priority for the new Council of Europe and, only eighteen months after the Statute was signed, the ten member States signed the Convention for the Protection of Human Rights and Fundamental Freedoms (European Convention on Human Rights) on 4 November 1950. The Convention entered into force on 3 September 1953.

2. The European Convention on Human Rights

The European Convention on Human Rights did not develop in a vacuum: it was preceded by both the Universal Declaration of Human Rights and the American Declaration of the Rights and Duties of Man. The Universal Declaration was in fact given pride of place in the Preamble to the Convention. The importance of the Convention to the protection of human rights at the international level should not be underestimated, however. In its Preamble, the Convention sets forth important principles:

[T]he foundation of justice and peace in the world... are best maintained on the one hand by an effective political democracy and on the other by a common understanding and observance of the Human Rights upon which they depend;

...

[T]he Governments of European countries which are likeminded and have a common heritage of political traditions, ideals, freedom and the rule of law ... take the first steps for the collective enforcement of certain of the Rights stated in the Universal Declaration.

Thus, the Preamble included the notion of political democracy that was lacking in the relevant provisions of the Statute of the Council of Europe. Of equal significance, however, is its focus on the collective enforcement of human rights.

The Convention was the first international human rights instrument to aspire to protect a broad range of civil and political rights both by taking the form of a treaty legally binding on its High Contracting Parties and by establishing a system of supervision over the implementation of the rights at the domestic level. Its most revolutionary contribution perhaps lay in its inclusion of a provision under which a High Contracting Party could choose to accept the supervision of the European Court of Human Rights in instances where an individual, rather than a State, initiated the process. One measure of the Convention's success has been the entrenchment of the right of individual petition as mandatory rather than optional: all States ratifying the Convention are now automatically bound to accept the jurisdiction of the Court to review individual complaints.

Chapter 1 – Article 1 of the Convention

Article 1

> The High Contracting Parties shall secure to everyone within their jurisdiction the rights and freedoms defined in Section I of this Convention.

Article 1 of the Convention introduces another important new element into international human rights law, by providing that the High Contracting Parties shall secure the rights and freedoms defined by the Convention to "everyone within their jurisdiction". The expression "everyone", like similar expressions to be found in other relevant international texts, emphasises the universal nature of the human rights recognised by the Convention: the Convention protects not just the rights of citizens, but also those of aliens, stateless persons, and persons lacking legal capacity, such as children or the severely disabled.

States that ratify the Convention automatically accept a two-fold obligation under Article 1. First, they must ensure that their domestic law is compatible with the Convention. This requirement, coupled with the prohibition of Article 57 against reservations of a general character, implies that ratifying States must meet this obligation from the moment of entry into force. In some instances, they may need to make certain adjustments to their law and practice in order to meet this obligation. Second, newly ratifying States must remedy any breach of the substantive rights and freedoms protected by the Convention.

The expression, "within their jurisdiction" seems to limit the number of people covered by the Convention, but in fact it only serves to establish a necessary link between "everyone" and the member State. In other words, in order for the Convention to be applicable, it must be physically possible for the State to secure the rights proclaimed. It is not necessary for a stable legal relationship to be established, such as "nationality", "residence" or "domicile"; it is sufficient for the State to be able to exercise a certain power in respect of the individual. Although there are 45 High Contracting Parties to the Convention, there have to date been nationals from over 150 countries filing petitions with the European Commission or Court of Human Rights. In some respects, however, a State may define its own jurisdiction, albeit always with regard to the confines of international law, including the relevant Articles of the Convention. For example, Article 56 permits a High Contracting Party to extend coverage of the Convention to "all or any of the territories for whose international relations it is responsible".

Article 1 of the Convention is a framework provision that cannot be breached on its own (*Streletz, Kessler and Krenz v. Germany* (2001) and *K.-H.W. v. Germany* (2001)).

Chapter 2 – The right to life: Article 2 and Protocols Nos. 6 and 13

Convention – Article 2

1. Everyone's right to life shall be protected by law. No one shall be deprived of his life intentionally save in the execution of a sentence of a court following his conviction of a crime for which this penalty is provided by law.

2. Deprivation of life shall not be regarded as inflicted in contravention of this Article when it results from the use of force which is no more than absolutely necessary:

a. in defence of any person from unlawful violence;

b. in order to effect a lawful arrest or to prevent the escape of a person lawfully detained;

c. in action lawfully taken for the purpose of quelling a riot or insurrection.

Protocol No. 6 (Substantive provisions)

1. The death penalty shall be abolished. No one shall be condemned to such penalty or executed.

2. A State may make provision in its law for the death penalty in respect of acts committed in time of war or of imminent threat of war; such penalty shall be applied only in the instances laid down in the law and in accordance with its provisions. The State shall communicate to the Secretary General of the Council of Europe the relevant provisions of that law.

3. No derogation from the provisions of this Protocol shall be made under Article 15 of the Convention.

4. No reservation may be made under Article 57 of the Convention in respect of the provisions of this Protocol.

Protocol No. 13 (Substantive provisions)

1. The death penalty shall be abolished. No one shall be condemned to such penalty or executed.

2. No derogation from the provisions of this Protocol shall be made under Article 15 of the Convention.

3. No reservation may be made under Article 57 of the Convention in respect of the provisions of this Protocol.

The right to life is certainly one of the most obvious basic human rights. That being said, it is important to note that neither Article 2, which establishes the right, nor Protocols Nos. 6 or 13, which call for the abolition of the death penalty, purport either to protect unconditionally life itself or to guarantee a certain quality of life. Instead, these provisions aim to protect the individual against any arbitrary deprivation of life by the State (*McCann and Others v. the*

United Kingdom (1995)) or any killing that may have resulted from the use of force by a private party (*Ergi v. Turkey* (1998) and *Yaşa v. Turkey* (1998)). The protection comprises both substantive and procedural elements.

1. Intentional deprivation of life

Article 2(1) states that "everyone's right to life shall be protected by law". In practical terms, this means that States must implement legislation criminalising intentional killings by private individuals and must guarantee that both the laws and the judicial system respond in a serious way to unlawful killings. For example, the Court found a violation of Article 2 where a number of individuals died as the result of an accident at a municipal rubbish dump. The responsible authorities were convicted of "negligence in the performance of their duties" and sentenced to pay a very small fine. Although the proceedings found that the authorities had been aware of the dangers posed by the rubbish dump prior to the accident, no consideration was given to allegations that they had endangered life (*Öneryildiz v. Turkey* (2002)). State obligations under Article 2 may also encompass other actions such as regulating hospitals and ensuring that the judicial system allows for the cause of a patient's death to be determined and for those responsible to be held accountable (*Calvelli and Ciglio v. Italy* (2002)).

In some instances, a State may have an affirmative obligation to protect individuals whom other individuals have threatened with violence, although any such positive obligation must be interpreted in a way which does not impose an impossible or disproportionate burden on the authorities (see, for example, *Osman v. the United Kingdom* (1998); *Akkoç v. Turkey* (2000) and *Kiliç v. Turkey* (2000)).

In addition to the capital punishment exception of Article 2(1), Article 2(2) provides for three additional, albeit circumscribed, exceptions to the prohibition against the intentional deprivation of life. The first is in defence of any person from unlawful violence, the second is in effecting a lawful arrest or preventing the escape of a detainee, and the third is in quelling a riot or insurrection. The principle governing the exercise of State discretion in applying any of these exceptions is that any force used must be "no more than [is] absolutely necessary", a stricter and more compelling standard for the assessment of the proportionality of State actions than appears under other Articles in the Convention (see Chapter 8 below). The Court has held that the notion of the "use of force" in Article 2 is not limited to the use of weapons or physical violence, but extends to such potentially lethal practices as the use of an army vehicle to break down a barricade (*McShane v. the United Kingdom* (2002)).

2. Substantive aspects of the right to life

Governmental actions involving the use of force outside the detention context

The European Court of Human Rights has reviewed a number of cases claiming that inadequate organisation and control of police or military operations had resulted in killings that contravened the requirements of Article 2 of the Convention. In the first case in which the Court found a violation of Article 2, *McCann and Others v. the United Kingdom* (1995) (three active members of the Irish Republican Army (IRA) shot and killed by members of British security forces in Gibraltar), the Court held that although the soldiers had acted on the honest belief that the killings were necessary in order to protect the lives of others, the organisation and control of the operation as a whole and, in particular, the United Kingdom Government's assessment and transmission of information to the soldiers at the time of the killings was inadequate. Since the McCann case, the Court has found a number of violations in cases in which killings have occurred as a result of inadequate organisation of governmental agents (see, for example, *Güleç v. Turkey* (1998) (individual killed by governmental security forces during a demonstration); *Ergi v. Turkey* (1998) (governmental security forces planned and conducted an ambush in connection with which they had taken insufficient measures to protect civilians); *Oğur v. Turkey* (1999) (shooting of a night watchman during a military operation) and *Gül v. Turkey* (2000) (police shot and killed a man through an apartment door in the course of a search operation)). In contrast, where a young couple were killed by a police officer in the course of a hostage rescue operation, the Court found that the organisation and conduct of the operation met the requirements of Article 2 (*Andronicou and Constantinou v. Cyprus* (1997)).

Governmental actions associated with deprivations of liberty

The State has an obligation to protect individuals who are in their custody or control as such persons are in a particularly vulnerable position with respect to the State. In particular, when an individual has been taken into police custody in good health and later dies, the State must give a plausible explanation of how the death transpired (*Velikova v. Bulgaria* (2000) and *Salman v. Turkey* (2000)).

Given the serious nature of any claim that the State has been responsible for the death of an individual in detention, the Court has established that the standard of proof when the Court assesses evidence is the "beyond a reasonable doubt" standard. In elaborating on this standard, however, the Court has stated:

> [S]uch proof may follow from the co-existence of sufficiently strong, clear and concordant inferences or of similar unrebutted presumptions of fact. Where the events in issue lie wholly, or in large part, within the exclusive knowledge of the authorities, as in the case of persons within their control in custody, strong presumptions of fact will arise in respect of injuries and death occurring during that detention. Indeed, the burden of proof may be regarded as resting on the authorities to provide a satisfactory and convincing explanation. (*Salman v. Turkey* (2000), paragraph 100)

As with police and military operations generally, States are required to exercise a duty of care towards individuals in detention beyond preventing their deaths through the active use of force by governmental agents. The Court found violations of Article 2 where a detainee was killed in an explosion while showing security forces the location of an ammunition dump (*Demiray v. Turkey* (2000)) and where a young man was stamped and kicked to death by a mentally ill detainee with a history of convictions and periods in psychiatric detention whom the authorities had placed in the same cell (*Paul and Audrey Edwards v. the United Kingdom* (2002)).

The Court found no violation of Article 2 where two men on leave from prison under a semi-custodial regime murdered the applicant's son. The Court considered that the system under which the individuals had been granted leave contained a number of safeguards intended to provide sufficient protective measures for society and thus the system itself could not be considered to be incompatible with Article 2. The men had also been convicted of the murder, sentenced to long prison terms and ordered to pay damages to the applicant. The Court thus did not consider that the measures taken by the authorities had given rise to any failure to protect the life of the applicant's son (*Mastromatteo v. Italy* (2002)).

3. Procedural aspects of the right to life

Effectiveness of governmental investigations

Even in cases in which agents responsible for unlawful deaths or killings cannot be identified, the Court will often find a violation of Article 2 on the basis of an ineffective investigation or the total lack of an investigation by the authorities. The essential purpose of such an investigation is to secure the effective implementation of the domestic laws which protect the right to life and to ensure the accountability of those responsible for unlawful deaths. The obligation for the authorities to undertake such an investigation is a unilateral obligation that arises on the authorities' becoming aware that an unlawful death or killing has transpired. In other words, no action should be required on the part of surviving relatives (see, for example, *İlhan v. Turkey* (2000) and *Kelly and Others v. the United Kingdom* (2001)).

The Court has established four main criteria for evaluating whether or not a governmental investigation into an alleged unlawful killing is "effective" as a partial safeguard of the right to life under Article 2. First, those investigating the allegations of an unlawful killing must be independent from those implicated in the events at issue (*Güleç v. Turkey* (1998) and *Oğur v. Turkey* (1999)). This means that not only must there be a lack of a hierarchical or institutional connection between these parties but there also must be independence in the fact-finding process itself (*Ergi v. Turkey* (1998) (violation where the public prosecutor had depended very heavily on information provided to him by the gendarmes who were implicated in the incident under investigation); (*McShane v. the United Kingdom* (2002) (violation where the investigation was conducted by police officers connected, albeit indirectly, with the operation under investigation)).

The second criterion of effectiveness distinguishes between obligations of result and obligations of conduct. Clearly a State's obligation to guarantee the right to life cannot realistically be interpreted to require that every unlawful killing result in a criminal conviction – not all murder cases can be solved. However, the Court has held that a State does have an obligation to guarantee that every investigation into an unlawful killing must be capable of leading to a determination of whether the force used was or was not justified in the circumstances *and* to the identification and punishment of those responsible. The Court has not accepted governmental arguments that the prosecution of some individuals for unlawful killings absolves the government from pursuing its own agents, where the substance of the claim under Article 2 is that the unlawful killings were carried out under governmental auspices or with their knowledge and acquiescence (*Avşar v. Turkey* (2001)). The Court has also established that "[a]ny deficiency in the investigation which undermines its ability to establish the cause of death or the person responsible will risk falling foul of this standard" (see, for example, *McShane v. the United Kingdom* (2002) (investigative body could not compel certain witnesses to testify at inquest into unlawful deaths, inquest could not yield a verdict or other means by which perpetrators could be identified and prosecuted); *Salman v. Turkey* (2000) and *Gül v. Turkey* (2000) (inadequate autopsies considered to undermine the effectiveness of any investigation into allegedly unlawful deaths)).

The third criterion of effectiveness is the promptness of the authorities in investigating a use of lethal force. The Court has noted that prompt action by the authorities is essential for maintaining public confidence in their adherence to the rule of law and in preventing any appearance of collusion in or tolerance of unlawful acts (*Avşar v. Turkey* (2001) and *McShane v. the United Kingdom* (2002)).

The fourth criterion of effectiveness is the sufficiency of public scrutiny of the investigation, and in particular, the opportunities of the next of kin to be involved in the investigative process to the extent necessary to safeguard their legitimate interests (*Shanaghan v. the United Kingdom* (2001) (family not provided with information about the conduct or progress of the investigation into their relative's death, including at the stage when the public prosecutor decided not to proceed with any prosecution) and *Kelly and Others v. the United Kingdom* (2001) (counsel for applicants refused access to witness statements used at the inquest)).

Effectiveness of remedies

In most cases raising claims of violations of the procedural aspects of Article 2 the Court has focused on the effectiveness of investigations conducted with a view to the criminal prosecution of those responsible for alleged unlawful killings. However, the Court has also held that in certain circumstances civil or administrative remedies may provide adequate protection where liability may be established and redress afforded through such channels (*Calvelli and Ciglio v. Italy* (2002) (medical negligence) and *Paul and Audrey Edwards v. the United Kingdom* (2002) (negligence by public authorities)). Delays in the payment of any compensation awarded through civil or administrative proceedings may also contribute to a finding of a violation of the procedural aspects of Article 2 (*Öneryildiz v. Turkey* (2002)).

4. Disappearances

In recent years, the European Court of Human Rights has been called upon to consider violations of Article 2 in cases in which individuals have disappeared after having been taken into the custody or control of the government. This group of cases can be broken into two rough categories, those in which documentation or other proof exists that an individual was detained by the authorities prior to his or her disappearance and those in which no such documentation or evidence exists.

In the former category of cases, the Court often finds violations of both the substantive and the procedural aspects of Article 2. The substantive violation will be based on the principle that where sufficient circumstantial evidence exists to support the conclusion that the individual disappeared whilst under the control of governmental agents, the authorities must provide a plausible explanation as to his or her fate, whether or not a body has been found. The procedural violation normally stems from the failure of the State to meet the criteria outlined above (see, for example, *Çakici v. Turkey* (1999), *Ertak v. Turkey* (2000) and *Çiçek v. Turkey* (2001)).

In the latter group of cases, the Court may only find a violation of the procedural aspects of Article 2 as it is normally impossible to establish the responsibility of governmental agents for the presumed death of the individual who has disappeared (see, for example, *Tanrıkulu v. Turkey* (1999)). In this respect, it is worth noting that the Court found a continuing violation of the procedural aspects of Article 2 in the case of *Cyprus v. Turkey* (2001), where the Respondent Government had failed for many years to investigate the fate of thousands of persons who had been placed in the custody and control of Turkish military troops in northern Cyprus and had subsequently disappeared.

5. The right to die

The right to life does not encompass the right to die. In the case of *Pretty v. the United Kingdom* (2002), the Court found no violation of Article 2 where the State refused to give an undertaking not to prosecute a man should he assist in the suicide of his wife, who was suffering from an incurable degenerative disease that affected all her physical functions but left her intellectual capacities unimpaired.

6. Abolition of the death penalty

Article 2(1) permits States to provide for capital punishment under certain conditions. However, Protocol No. 6 to the Convention calls for the abolition of the death penalty except in extremely narrow circumstances. (As of 31 December 2003, forty-three countries had ratified Protocol No. 6.) Protocol No. 13, which calls for the abolition of the death penalty in all circumstances, entered into force in July 2003. (As of 31 December 2003, twenty countries had ratified Protocol No. 13.)

Chapter 3 – Torture, inhuman or degrading treatment or punishment: Article 3

Article 3

> No one shall be subjected to torture or to inhuman or degrading treatment or punishment.

The rights protected under Article 3 of the Convention relate directly to an individual's personal integrity and human dignity. Freedom from torture, inhuman or degrading treatment or punishment are therefore rights of an extremely serious nature. They are non-derogable rights under Article 15 of the Convention.

The European Court of Human Rights has differentiated amongst the three substantive concepts in Article 3 in terms of the degree of severity of particular treatments or punishments in the case of *Ireland v. the United Kingdom* (1978):

> torture: deliberate inhuman treatment causing very serious and cruel suffering;

> inhuman treatment or punishment: the infliction of intense physical and mental suffering;

> degrading treatment: ill-treatment designed to arouse in victims feelings of fear, anguish and inferiority capable of humiliating and debasing them and possibly breaking their physical or moral resistance.

1. Torture

Torture is the most extreme degree of ill-treatment prohibited under the European Convention on Human Rights. Some examples of the types of cases in which the Court has found torture include those in which an individual had been subjected to "Palestinian hanging" (being stripped naked and suspended for long periods of time by the arms, which had been tied together behind his back) (*Aksoy v. Turkey* (1996)); raped while in police custody (*Aydin v. Turkey* (1997)); severely beaten, dragged by the hair, urinated on and threatened with a blow torch and a syringe (*Selmouni v. France* (1999)); and subjected to electric shocks, hot and cold water treatment, blows to the head and threats to ill-treat her children (*Akkoç v. Turkey* (2000)). Although torture may be inflicted on someone for the purpose of extracting a confession or information, as occurred in the case of *Dikme v. Turkey* (2000), the Court has not found such a motive to be a necessary element in finding that torture has occurred.

2. Inhuman or degrading treatment or punishment

Although torture invariably occurs in the context of detention, the Court has found violations of the prohibition against inhuman or degrading treatment both within and outside the detention context.

Inhuman or degrading treatment or punishment in the context of detention

Active physical abuse of detainees

The Court has found a number of substantive violations of Article 3 in cases in which individuals have been ill-treated in detention. In the cases of *Tomasi v. France* (1992) and *Ribitsch v. Austria* (1995), the Court found violations of Article 3 where the individuals submitted timely documentation about injuries allegedly suffered whilst in police custody and where the governments offered no credible alternative explanation as to the cause of those injuries. In the former case, the Court also stressed that the fight against organised crime or terrorism could not be invoked as a justification for the ill-treatment of a detainee. In the latter case, the Court established the principle that any recourse to physical force that was not necessitated strictly by the detainee's own conduct was in principle an infringement of Article 3. Such conduct would not include the refusal to submit to a search procedure prior to appearing in court (*Satik and Others v. Turkey* (2000) (applicants beaten by prison staff and gendarmes on those grounds)).

It is incumbent on the State to ensure that force applied to an individual at the time of arrest also does not contravene the prohibition against ill-treatment (*Rehbock v. Slovenia* (2000) (violation where applicant's jaw was fractured during the course of his arrest)). The duty of the State to ensure that a detainee is not subjected to prohibited ill-treatment extends to the affirmative obligation to protect him or her from abuse by other detainees. In *Pantea v. Romania* (2003) a pre-trial detainee was seriously injured by repeat offender cell-mates with no intervention from the warden. After this incident, he was handcuffed whilst remaining in the same cell as his abusers and was forced to travel for several days standing up in a railway wagon having not received medical treatment for the several fractures he had suffered in the beating.

The Court has stressed that where an individual dies in custody, it is incumbent on the State to provide a satisfactory explanation for the cause of the death and, in particular, to maintain detailed and accurate records with respect to any injuries the individual had suffered (*Salman v. Turkey* (2000)).

General conditions in detention facilities

Until relatively recently, the European Court of Human Rights has been reluctant to find violations of Article 3 with respect to complaints about conditions in detention facilities, as opposed to complaints about physical abuse by authorities in such facilities. However, it has done so in cases in which a detainee was confined for at least two months in a very small unventilated cell with a toilet that was not screened from view (*Peers v. Greece* (2001)) and in an overcrowded and dirty cell with insufficient sanitary and sleeping facilities, no fresh air or natural daylight and nowhere to exercise (*Dougoz v. Greece* (2001)). In the case of *Kalashnikov v. Russia* (2002), the applicant had been detained in a seventeen metre square cell with twenty-three other men. The lights and television in the cell were on twenty-four hours a day, with the prisoners forced to sleep in shifts in those conditions. Hygienic conditions led to the development of serious health problems, resulting in some instances in the loss of fingernails or toenails. The Court found a violation of Article 3.

Conditions on "death row"

In most prisons in countries that still have the death penalty, individuals who have been condemned to death are often housed in separate facilities from the general prison population ("death row") and subjected to a very restrictive regime and other unfavourable conditions. These factors, plus the long period of time that a condemned prisoner could expect to stay on death row in the United States, led the Court to find that a violation of Article 3 would occur should the United Kingdom extradite a young German national to the United States to face charges of capital murder (*Soering v. the United Kingdom* (1989)).

The Court has found a number of violations of Article 3 with respect to conditions on death row in the Ukraine, which included prisoners being locked up for twenty-four hours a day in very small cells with no natural light, limited access to water and sanitary facilities, and no opportunity for outdoor exercise, other activities or human contact (see, for example, *Poltoratskiy v. Ukraine* (2003) and *Kuznetsov v. Ukraine* (2003)).

Inappropriate treatment or practices in detention facilities

An individual in detention is totally dependent on governmental authorities to meet his or her most basic needs. This vulnerability of persons in detention engenders an obligation for the authorities to take into consideration the personal attributes and requirements of each detainee, both at the time of detention and throughout the period of time during which he or she is under governmental custody and control.

With respect to initial placements in detention facilities, the Court has held that the detention of a severely disabled person in conditions where she was dangerously cold, risked developing sores because her bed was too hard or unreachable, and was unable to go to the toilet or keep clean without the greatest of difficulty, constituted degrading treatment contrary to Article 3 (*Price v. the United Kingdom* (2001)).

In addition to finding violations of Article 3 where authorities have actively abused detainees, the Court has also found violations of Article 3 where the provision of medical care or circumstances surrounding the provision of such care constituted inhuman or degrading treatment (see, for example, *McGlinchey and Others v. the United Kingdom* (2003) (inadequate medical care provided by prison authorities to heroin addict suffering from with-drawal symptoms); *Mouisel v. France* (2002) (detainee receiving treatment for cancer constantly shackled, forced to undergo intimate medical procedures, and not provided with appropriate accommodation)).

The Court has also found violations of Article 3 where a male detainee was strip searched, including an examination of his genitals, in the presence of a woman (*Valašinas v. Lithuania* (2001)) and where the detention regime in a maximum security prison included regular strip searches (*Van der Ven v. the Netherlands* (2003)).

The Court has also examined several cases raising issues claiming violations of Article 3 due to inappropriate or inadequate supervision of the conditions of detention, given the personal circumstances of the detainee. In the case of *Keenan v. the United Kingdom* (2001), the parents of a young man who committed suicide while serving a four-month prison sentence successfully alleged that his rights under Article 3 had been violated due to the lack both of effective monitoring of his condition and of informed psychiatric input, coupled with the imposition of prison disciplinary punishment.

Individuals detained on the grounds of mental illness or other psychiatric problems have sometimes claimed that the involuntary imposition of medical or other treatment is in contravention of Article 3. In the case of *Herczegfalvy v. Austria* (1992), the Court held that a measure which is a therapeutic necessity cannot be regarded as inhuman or degrading in the sense of the Convention.

Inhuman or degrading treatment or punishment outside the detention context

Destruction of homes and possessions

Consistent with its case-law under Article 2, in examining allegations of violations of Article 3 the Court has minimised its consideration of the motives or intentions of a State whose actions have been called into question. For example, where governmental authorities violently and deliberately burned the homes of the applicants, in their presence and disregarding their safety as they tried to retrieve their personal belongings, and subsequently providing them with no assistance, the Court did not find it necessary to inquire about any justification the government might offer for such actions, finding that the actions constituted inhuman treatment in the sense of Article 3 (*Selçuk and Asker v. Turkey* (1998)).

Forcible expulsions

The threshold of "deliberate infliction of severe physical and mental suffering" was also reached in the case of *Denizci and Others v. Cyprus* (2001). In this case, the Cypriot Government had forcibly expelled a number of ethnic Turks to the northern part of the island, the police conducting the operation seriously injuring some of the expellees. The Court considered that the conduct of the operation constituted inhuman treatment.

Protection of juveniles

The Court has held that the obligations of the State under Article 3 extend to protecting individuals from ill-treatment by private parties as well as ill-treatment by governmental authorities. In the case of *A. v. the United Kingdom* (1998), the Court found that the failure of English law adequately to protect the applicant from ill-treatment by his stepfather constituted a violation of Article 3; and in the case of *Z and Others v. the United Kingdom* (2001), the Court found a violation of Article 3 where local authorities had failed to take adequate protective measures in respect of severe neglect and abuse suffered by several children due to ill-treatment by their parents over the course of many years. It is important to note that the governmental authorities in both of these cases were fully apprised of the circumstances of the applicants and had failed to take adequate action to prevent further abuse.

In the case of *Tyrer v. the United Kingdom* (1978), a juvenile offender had been sentenced in the Isle of Man to be birched. The Court held that such institutionalised violence placed the offender in a position where his dignity and physical integrity were compromised, through treating him as "an object in the power of the authorities".

3. Extradition and expulsion

An individual occasionally claims that a State's action to extradite or expel him to another State where he may be subjected to torture, inhuman or degrading treatment constitutes a violation of Article 3 (see above-mentioned case of *Soering v. the United Kingdom* (1989)). In recent years, the Court has expanded on the idea that sending an individual to a country in which he or she might well face prohibited ill-treatment may lead to a violation of Article 3. Stressing the unconditional nature of the prohibition against ill-treatment, the Court has established the principle that a state wishing to deport even an individual found guilty of a serious criminal offence (*Ahmed v. Austria* (1996)) or constituting a threat to national security (*Chahal v. the United Kingdom* (1996)) must nevertheless make an independent evaluation of the circumstances the individual would face in the country of return.

Although in general both States Parties and the Convention organs will primarily consider political factors in the country of return when evaluating whether a particular deportation might constitute a violation of Article 3, in one case the Court found a violation where the lack of emotional or financial support and the poor quality of medical care in the country of return was inadequate to meet the needs of an individual in the final stages of Aids (*D. v. the United Kingdom* (1997)). In another, it found a violation where a woman would face the risk of being stoned to death for adultery if she were to be deported back to her country of origin (*Jabari v. Turkey* (2000)).

4. Relatives of persons who have disappeared

In recent years, the Court has found that relatives of alleged victims of serious human rights violations may raise claims of ill-treatment on their own behalves as well as those of their relatives. Thus, even if it may be impossible to establish whether an individual suffered ill-treatment at the hands of the authorities, the uncertainty surrounding their fate may engender an independent violation of Article 3. The Court has found violations of Article 3 in such cases where one or more close relatives have disappeared in circumstances engaging the responsibility of the State and where the governmental authorities have failed to ascertain their fate or to treat survivors' requests for information in a timely and sensitive way. The Court considers that the fear and anguish suffered by those not knowing what had happened to their loved ones, sometimes for years, reaches the threshold of inhuman and degrading treatment prohibited under Article 3 (see, for example, *Kurt v. Turkey* (1998), *Taş v. Turkey* (2000) and *Çiçek v. Turkey* (2001)).

5. Discrimination as prohibited ill-treatment

On occasions, the Court has reviewed complaints that a State has instituted widespread policies and practices that have such negative effects on one part of the population as to constitute prohibited ill-treatment under Article 3 of the Convention. In the case of *Cyprus v. Turkey* (2001), the Applicant Government documented a pattern of discriminatory treatment of Greek Cypriots living in the Karpas area of northern Cyprus, including severe restrictions on the exercise of basic freedoms, for example, the right to bequeath immovable property to a relative unless the relative also lived in the north, the right of Greek Cypriot children in the area to education to the same level as Turkish Cypriot children in the absence of secondary schools and the effective prohibition of return for those educated elsewhere, and the right to freedom of movement affecting freedom of religion and association. The Court found that "[t]he conditions under which [the subject population] is condemned to live are debasing and violate the very notion of respect for the human dignity of its members" and held that the nature and duration of the discriminatory practices attained a level of severity which amounted to degrading treatment prohibited under Article 3 of the Convention.

6. Procedural aspects of the prohibition against ill-treatment

The Court takes the same approach to evaluating procedural aspects of claims of violations of Article 3 as it does with respect to those under Article 2. In particular, if the Court is unable to determine if alleged ill-treatment in fact occurred (substantive violation), it nevertheless will make an independent assessment of the adequacy of the government's response to the allegations (procedural violation). For example, in cases in which individuals allege that they have been ill-treated whilst in detention, the Court may find it impossible to determine the facts, but it may nevertheless find a violation of Article 3 if official investigations of the allegations do not meet required standards of effectiveness (*Assenov and Others v. Bulgaria* (1998) and *Labita v. Italy* (2000)).

Chapter 4 – Slavery and forced labour: Article 4

Article 4

1. No one shall be held in slavery or servitude.

2. No one shall be required to perform forced or compulsory labour.

3. For the purpose of this Article the term "forced or compulsory labour" shall not include:

    a. any work required to be done in the ordinary course of detention imposed according to the provisions of Article 5 of this Convention or during conditional release from such detention;

    b. any service of a military character or, in case of conscientious objectors in countries where they are recognised, service exacted instead of compulsory military service;

    c. any service exacted in case of an emergency or calamity threatening the life or well-being of the community;

    d. any work or service which forms part of normal civic obligations.

Article 4 of the Convention addresses slavery and servitude separately from forced and compulsory labour. The two former terms encompass far-reaching forms of control over the individual and characterise oppressive conditions which the individual cannot change and from which there is no escape. The two latter terms focus on the involuntary nature of particular work or services, to be performed on a temporary basis or as an adjunct to other obligations or civil circumstances.

Article 4(1): Slavery and servitude

The Convention institutions have reviewed few cases raising claims of violation of the prohibition against slavery or servitude found in Article 4(1). Most such claims have been raised by prisoners, with a uniform lack of success.

In the case of *Van Droogenbroeck v. Belgium* (1982), a recidivist who had been placed at the disposal of the administrative authorities complained that being subjected to such supervision constituted prohibited servitude under Article 4(1). The Court disagreed, noting that the restrictive measures were both of limited duration and subject to judicial supervision. It further noted that the measure did not affect the applicant's legal status to the extent required to meet the slavery or servitude standard.

In the case of *W, X, Y and Z v. the United Kingdom* (Appl. Nos. 3435-3438/67), four young men, when fifteen or sixteen years old, had committed themselves to serve in the navy for nine-year tours of duty. All had later applied for discharges and had been refused. In their application to the Commission, the four argued that in view of their age at the time of the original agreement the enforcement of that agreement constituted prohibited servitude under

Article 4(1). When declaring the application inadmissible, the Commission first noted that military service could be considered an exception to the prohibition against forced labour under Article 4(2), but could not be considered servitude under Article 4(1). It further found that because domestic legislation required the State to obtain the consent of the parents of minors wishing to enlist, and because such consent had been obtained in all four cases, the four young men were bound to complete their tours. The Commission specifically noted that consent deprives work or service of its compulsory character.

Article 4(2): Forced or compulsory labour

The Convention institutions have reviewed several cases raising issues under Article 4(2), which prohibits forced or compulsory labour, and Article 4(3), which sets forth exceptions to this general prohibition. Instead of arriving at independent definitions for the term "forced or compulsory labour", the Court has applied the definitions provided in the relevant conventions of the International Labour Organization. For example, in the case of *Van der Mussele v. Belgium* (1983) a young Belgian barrister complained that the obligation to represent indigent defendants, without being compensated for the work or reimbursed for expenditures incurred, constituted a violation of Article 4(2). The Court began its review by citing Article 2 of ILO Convention No. 29, which defines "compulsory labour" as "all work or service which is exacted from any person under the menace of any penalty and for which the said person has not offered himself voluntarily". In finding no violation of Article 4(2), the Court noted the following factors, among others: that the work was not outside the scope of normal duties for a barrister, that provision of the services contributed to professional development, and that the amount of work was not too burdensome. The Court also pointed out that the Belgian system of appointed counsel for indigents was both one means of guaranteeing the right to counsel under Article 6(3)(c) of the Convention and "a normal civic obligation" under Article 4(3)(d).

As of the end of 2003, the Court had found a violation of the prohibition against forced or compulsory labour only once, and that in conjunction with the prohibition of discrimination, where a government required all male citizens either to serve in the fire brigade or to pay a fee in lieu of such service (*Karlheinz Schmidt v. Germany* (1994)).

The Commission declared inadmissible a number of applications in which members of various professions argued that the imposition of obligations on members of a given profession to provide services of a certain type or in a given location constituted a violation of Article 4(2) of the Convention. As might be expected, most of these applications were from members of the legal profession. In the Iversen case (Appl. No. 1468/62), however, a Norwegian dentist argued that being forced to provide services in an isolated part of the country, after concerted efforts to find a dentist willing to locate in the region had failed, constituted a violation of Article 4(2). Some Commission members found that such impressed service could be justified on the grounds set forth in Article 4(3)(c), "emergency or calamity threatening the life or well-being of the community". Others found that the limited time, the proper remuneration, and the nature of the services to be provided were consonant with the applicant's choice of profession.

The Commission also found inadmissible several cases raising issues under the provision of Article 4(3)(b) that excludes from the definition of "forced or compulsory labour" services required of conscientious objectors to military service, in those countries that recognise conscientious objection. This provision does not oblige any High Contracting Party either to recognise conscientious objection or to exempt conscientious objectors from serving in alternative employment for periods of time roughly equivalent to those served by military recruits.

Chapter 5 – Liberty and security of person: Article 5 and Articles 1 and 2 of Protocol No. 4

Convention – Article 5

1.   Everyone has the right to liberty and security of person. No one shall be deprived of his liberty save in the following cases and in accordance with a procedure prescribed by law:

   a.   the lawful detention of a person after conviction by a competent court;

   b.   the lawful arrest or detention of a person for non-compliance with the lawful order of a court or in order to secure the fulfilment of any obligation prescribed by law;

   c.   the lawful arrest or detention of a person effected for the purpose of bringing him before the competent legal authority on reasonable suspicion of having committed an offence or when it is reasonably considered necessary to prevent his committing an offence or fleeing after having done so;

   d.   the detention of a minor by lawful order for the purpose of educational supervision or his lawful detention for the purpose of bringing him before the competent legal authority;

   e.   the lawful detention of persons for the prevention of the spreading of infectious diseases, of persons of unsound mind, alcoholics or drug addicts or vagrants;

   f.   the lawful arrest or detention of a person to prevent his effecting an unauthorised entry into the country or of a person against whom action is being taken with a view to deportation or extradition.

2.   Everyone who is arrested shall be informed promptly, in a language which he understands, of the reasons for his arrest and of any charge against him.

3.   Everyone arrested or detained in accordance with the provisions of paragraph 1.c. of this Article shall be brought promptly before a judge or other officer authorised by law to exercise judicial power and shall be entitled to trial within a reasonable time or to release pending trial. Release may be conditioned by guarantees to appear for trial.

4.   Everyone who is deprived of his liberty by arrest or detention shall be entitled to take proceedings by which the lawfulness of his detention shall be decided speedily by a court and his release ordered if the detention is not lawful.

5.   Everyone who has been the victim of arrest or detention in contravention of the provisions of this Article shall have an enforceable right to compensation.

Protocol No. 4 – Article 1

No one shall be deprived of his liberty merely on the ground of inability to fulfil a contractual obligation.

Protocol No. 4 – Article 2

1. Everyone lawfully within the territory of a State shall, within that territory, have the right to liberty of movement and freedom to choose his residence.

2. Everyone shall be free to leave any country, including his own.

3. No restrictions shall be placed on the exercise of these rights other than such as are in accordance with law and are necessary in a democratic society in the interests of national security or public safety, for the maintenance of *ordre public*, for the prevention of crime, for the protection of health or morals, or for the protection of the rights and freedoms of others.

4. The rights set forth in paragraph 1 may also be subject, in particular areas, to restrictions imposed in accordance with law and justified by the public interest in a democratic society.

Article 5(1) of the Convention secures to everyone the right to liberty and security of person, save in six types of circumstances which are delineated in the rest of the provision and which provide an exhaustive list of exceptions to the general rule. In other words, a High Contracting Party does not have the discretion to create additional categories of justification for detaining or imprisoning individuals, but must act within the confines established by the Convention. Furthermore, the Court interprets even the exceptions narrowly, holding that only this approach is consistent with the aims of the provision.

Article 5 as a whole contemplates the protection of physical liberty and particularly freedom from arbitrary arrest or detention. The Article does not afford protection against less serious forms of restriction on individual freedom, such as the implementation of traffic regulations, the required registration of aliens or citizens, the operation of curfews, or other types of control that do not seriously restrict an individual's freedom to move about in the community. However, where a custodial parent had committed a twelve-year-old child to a psychiatric hospital, the Court held that Article 5 did not apply (*Nielsen v. Denmark* (1988)). Where the competent authorities had placed an elderly woman suffering from senile dementia in a foster home, the Court also found the Article inapplicable (*H. M. v. Switzerland* (2002)).

In a few cases, individuals have complained about the type of facilities in which they have been detained. The Court has found no violation of Article 5 where a State detained a convicted criminal in an ordinary prison and not in a prison with special medical facilities as ordered by a domestic court, noting that the primary purpose of the detention was punishment and not medical treatment (*Bizzotto v. Greece* (1996)). In contrast, in the case of *Aerts v. Belgium* (1998), the Court found a violation of Article 5(1) where the applicant had been held, for seven months of his total detention, in the psychiatric wing of an ordinary prison, rather than in a social protection centre designated by the competent mental health board.

1. Lawfulness under Article 5

As noted above, in order to be in compliance with Article 5, a government cannot detain someone for any reason other than those listed (whether or not there is a domestic legal provision that applies). That being said, however, where there is no domestic legal basis for a deprivation of liberty the Court will find a violation of Article 5 (see, for example, *Laumont v. France* (2001), *Baranowski v. Poland* (2000), *Quinn v. France* (1995), *Labita v. Italy* (2000) and *K.-F. v. Germany* (1997) (applicants kept in detention after the expiry of the relevant detention order and no other grounds existed that could justify the continuation of the detention), and *Tsirlis and Kouloumpas v. Greece* (1997) (two Jehovah's Witnesses ministers detained for their refusal to serve in the military, although domestic law recognised the Jehovah's Witnesses as a "known religion" and exempted ministers of known religions from military service)). In two more nuanced cases, the Court found a violation of Article 5 where the authorities co-operated in confining alleged members of a sect in a secure facility for deprogramming (*Riera Blume and Others v. Spain* (1999)) and where a member of parliament was detained for misappropriation of public funds on the grounds that he had participated in decisions granting aid to certain developing countries when a member of the government, but where no evidence was adduced to show that participation in such decision-making processes was unlawful or that the individual had benefited financially from the decisions taken (*Lukanov v. Bulgaria* (1997)).

The main attribute of the notion of "lawfulness" under Article 5 is to protect the individual from being deprived of his or her liberty on unfounded grounds or in an arbitrary way (*N.C. v. Italy* (2002) and *Winterwerp v. the Netherlands* (1979)). The Court interprets the notion of "lawfulness" autonomously, taking the applicable domestic law only as a starting point, but reviewing that domestic law and/or its application in light of the broader criteria for "lawfulness" established under the Convention case-law (see Chapters 7 and 8 below). In developing this principle in the context of Article 5, the Court has held that there will be a violation where domestic law and practice allow for legal presumptions that an individual who has been indicted on serious criminal charges will abscond if not detained, where the law prescribes mandatory detention if an individual has previously been convicted of a criminal offence (*Caballero v. the United Kingdom* (2000)) or where the judicial authority determining the necessity for detention makes pro forma invocations of such grounds for ordering detention as the "state of the evidence", without providing further argumentation.

The case-law of the Court establishes that the question of whether an individual has been deprived of his or her liberty in violation of Article 5 must be determined on a case-by-case basis, taking into account all the circumstances of the individual case. Thus, in the case of *Engel and Others v. the Netherlands* (1976), the Court found that restricting soldiers to their barracks does not run afoul of Article 5 where such restrictions were "not beyond the exigencies of normal military service", whereas the same types of restrictions on civilians would be unacceptable. For example, in the case of *Lavents v. Latvia* (2002), the Court held that "house arrest" constituted a deprivation of liberty in the sense of Article 5. In the case of *Guzzardi v. Italy* (1980), the Court held that an individual forced to stay within a small area on an island and limited as to the types and numbers of his social contacts could be considered to be deprived of his liberty.

Normally, the Court will find that for a deprivation of liberty to be lawful, a court order or, for a brief and reviewable period of time, a prosecutor's order is required; and, in order to preclude the possibility of arbitrary detentions, any deprivation of liberty must be amenable to independent judicial scrutiny and must secure the accountability of the authorities for any measures taken. In the case of *Denizci and Others v. Cyprus* (2001), the applicants were arrested, kept in custody by Cypriot police officers and then expelled to northern Cyprus. During the course of this operation, they were given neither reasons, a court order, a judgment or an arrest warrant that would have provided them with information about the grounds for their detention. The Court found that the unlawfulness of their initial arrest tainted the entire period of their entire subsequent detention.

2. Detention in the criminal context

Article 5(1) provides that a State may legitimately detain someone on grounds founded in either the criminal or the civil law. Deprivations of liberty governed by Article 5(1)(a) and 5(1)(c) fall within the realm of the criminal law.

Detention after a criminal conviction: Article 5(1)(a)

Article 5(1)(a) provides that the State may detain an individual after his or her conviction by a competent court. The purpose of Article 5 is to protect an individual against *arbitrary* detention: it does not prohibit detention itself. It follows that an individual who has been convicted in first instance proceedings may be detained during the course of any appeals process. However, the Court has found that continued detention is not acceptable where prison authorities take an administrative decision to lengthen a prisoner's detention for alleged commission of a triable offence (*Van Droogenbroeck v. Belgium* (1982)).

Detention on remand: Article 5(1)(c)

The main operative standard of Article 5(1)(c) is reasonableness. The Court has held that in order for a deprivation of liberty to meet the standards dictated under the "reasonable suspicion" provision of Article 5(1)(c), the State is not required to establish guilt. In fact, the provision does not even presuppose that the police have already obtained sufficient evidence to bring charges, either at the point of arrest or while the applicant is detained at the initial stages of an investigation (*Ergadöz v. Turkey* (1997)). However, the State must base arrest and detention in this early phase of criminal investigation on at least some threshold level of facts or information substantiating the suspicion that an offence has been committed and that the detainee has a sufficient connection with the commission of the offence at issue.

Generally categorising someone as a terrorist is not sufficient under Article 5(1)(c) (*Fox, Campbell and Hartley v. the United Kingdom* (1990)). In contrast, if an individual is detained on the grounds that he or she is in a position to further police investigations into facts and circumstances on which concrete suspicions are grounded, detention may be acceptable under this provision (*Brogan v. the United Kingdom* (1988)). In the first case ever reviewed by the Court, *Lawless v. Ireland* (1961), the Court held that a State could not detain a suspected terrorist without bringing him before a court and without intending to bring him to trial.

Under Article 5(1), grounds for detention must be both specific and lawful in the sense of the Convention. For example, Article 5 does not permit the detention of someone for the purposes of general social control or on the grounds of vague suspicions that the person being detained may be engaged in criminal activities (*Ječius v. Lithuania* (2000) (domestic law permitted detention for "preventive" purposes in connection with "banditism, criminal association and terrorising a person")). Nor does it permit detention on the basis of grounds not articulated in any formal decisions taken by the competent authorities (*Trzaska v. Poland* (2000)).

The Court has clearly established that the principles of legal certainty and the protection of individuals from arbitrariness require that any deprivation of liberty must not only have a specific legal basis, but also clear rules governing the detainee's situation. The Court has consistently held that for a deprivation of liberty to be acceptable under Article 5(1)(c) the existence of a suspicion is essential, but not sufficient as a ground to prolong detention after a certain lapse of time (*Stögmüller v. Austria* (1969)). Any deprivation of liberty for an unlimited period without judicial authorisation will be incompatible with these principles (*Baranowski v. Poland* (2000) (detention based on the practice of "placing a detainee at the disposal of the court"), *Kawka v. Poland* (2001) (detention based solely on the grounds that a bill of indictment had been submitted to the competent court) and *Grauslys v. Lithuania* (2000) (detention based on the fact that the case had been transmitted to court or that applicant had access to the case file)).

Any detention effected under Article 5(1)(c) is subject to judicial review under Article 5(3) at the outset of the deprivation of liberty and under Article 5(4) throughout the period of detention. In the latter respect, it is important to keep in mind that Article 5(3) comes into play only with respect to deprivations of liberty effected under Article 5(1)(c), whereas Article 5(4) applies to any deprivation of liberty, including in the civil context.

3. Detention in the civil context

Paragraphs (b), (d), (e) and (f) of Article 5(1) provide the complete list of circumstances in which an individual can be deprived of his or her liberty in the civil context.

Detention for the fulfilment of legal obligations: Article 5(1)(b)

Article 5(1)(b) permits detention to ensure that an individual fulfils "any obligation prescribed by law", for example, the payment of a community charge (*Perks and Others v. the United Kingdom* (1999)). The Court has held that any such obligation must be specific and concrete, not just a general obligation to observe the law (*Engel and Others v. the Netherlands* (1976) and *Lawless v. Ireland* (1961)) or to "change one's behaviour" (*Ciulla v. Italy* (1989)). Even if an individual may legitimately be detained for one of the purposes permitted under Article 5(1)(b), the manner in which the authorities exercise their powers vis-à-vis the individual may lead to the finding of a violation, if the method used is disproportionate to the obligation at issue (*Raninen v. Finland* (1997) (arrest, detention and handcuffing of military conscript objecting to military and substitute service) or if the authorities have failed to consider less restrictive means of addressing a particular problem than detention (*Witold Litwa v. Poland* (2000) (almost blind person detained in a sobering-up centre for six and a half hours after he allegedly disturbed public order whilst intoxicated, although domestic legislation set forth also other less onerous possibilities for handling the situation)).

It is important to note that Article 1 of Protocol No. 4 prohibits "deprivation of liberty merely on the ground of inability to fulfil a contractual obligation". No cases have arisen under this provision.

Detention of minors: Article 5(1)(d)

Article 5(1)(d) allows a High Contracting Party to detain a minor for the purpose of educational supervision or to bring him or her before the competent legal authority. There have been relatively few cases under this provision of the Convention. However, in both of the main cases (*Bouamar v. Belgium* (1988) and *D.G. v. Ireland* (2002)), the European Court of Human Rights found that each of the respective States had violated Article 5(1)(d) by justifying the detention of a minor on the grounds of "educational supervision" but actually detaining the minor in a prison or other facility in which such supervision could not or did not take place.

Detention of persons of unsound mind, vagrants, etc.: Article 5(1)(e)

Article 5(1)(e) permits detention for purposes of health and social control in a number of unrelated human situations. The majority of cases under this Article have contested detention in psychiatric hospitals. In the case of *Winterwerp v. the Netherlands* (1979), the Court set forth three criteria by which to judge the notion of "unsound mind" under Article 5(1)(e). First, the State must apply objective medical standards in determining whether an individual can be considered to be of unsound mind; second, the nature or degree of the unsoundness must be sufficiently extreme to justify detention; and third, the State may confine the individual only so long as the mental disorder persists. Implicit in the last criterion is the right to periodic review of detention grounded in the "unsound mind" provision: such detention cannot be for an indefinite period. The Court has held that Article 5(1)(e) does not require the State to provide any particular level of treatment in order to ensure that an individual detained under the "unsound mind" provision is detained no longer than absolutely necessary (*Winterwerp v. the Netherlands* (1979) and *Ashingdane v. the United Kingdom* (1985)). It does, however, require the State to comply with domestic decisions regarding the type of facility in which an individual is to be detained (see above-mentioned case of *Aerts v. Belgium* (1998)).

The State may not unduly delay the release from psychiatric detention of an individual who has been found to be no longer mentally ill pending the availability of a place in a community hostel providing special care. Where a government imposes such conditions on release, the government must undertake measures to secure those conditions (*Johnson v. the United Kingdom* (1997)).

The Court has reviewed a number of cases claiming violations of both Article 5(1)(e) and one or more of the procedural provisions of Article 5. In the case of *Van der Leer v. the Netherlands* (1990), the Court held that the Dutch Government violated Article 5(1), (2) and (4) in authorising the applicant's confinement in a psychiatric hospital without either informing her of the committal decision or soliciting her views on the matter. In the case of *Wassink v. the Netherlands* (1990), the Court held that a procedure whereby psychiatric confinement could be ordered on the basis of telephone interviews conformed to the requirements of Article 5, but that the absence of a registrar at the subsequent hearing was contrary to domestic law and thus violated the requirement of "lawfulness". In *Varbanov v. Bulgaria* (2000), the Court found a violation of Article 5(1)(e) where the applicant had been detained on the grounds of being of unsound mind by order of a public prosecutor with no reference to any assessment of mental disorder by an expert and of Article 5(4) for the absence of any procedure through which the applicant could challenge the deprivation of liberty.

Immigration-related deprivations of liberty: Article 5(1)(f)

Article 5(1)(f) permits detention in connection with immigration, asylum and extradition matters. At the outset, it is important to note that there is no right of political asylum under the European Convention on Human Rights. However, the requirement of "lawfulness" of Article 5(1) generally means that the High Contracting Parties may not act in an arbitrary manner in exercising their sovereign authority in any of the areas covered by this provision. In the case of *Bozano v. France* (1986), the Court found a violation of Article 5(1) where the French authorities purportedly had detained someone with a view to deportation, but in fact had done so with a view to circumventing restrictions on extradition. In the case of *Amuur v. France* (1996), the Court found a violation of the same general provision where several individuals who were seeking asylum were detained in the international departures area in a French airport for almost three weeks without any possibility of challenging their detention.

In the case of *Čonka v. Belgium* (2002), the Court found a violation of not only this provision but also of Article 4 of Protocol No. 4 (prohibiting the mass expulsion of aliens) where the Belgian authorities arrested the applicants with a view to their expulsion after they had been summoned to complete asylum requests; the Court held that the violation of the Convention was grounded in large part on the improper actions taken by the authorities (misrepresentations about the purpose of the summons and obstruction of the exercise of procedural rights). In the case of *Dougoz v. Greece* (2001), the Court found a violation where the public prosecutor had ordered the detention of an individual with a view to deportation after the body afforded competence to issue such orders by the domestic law had stated that detention was not necessary.

There is no time limit for permissible detentions under Article 5(1)(f) although the procedural protections afforded under Article 5(4) must be available and effective (see, for example, *Chahal v. the United Kingdom* (1996) (Sikh separatist detained for six years pending execution of a deportation order to India for national security reasons)).

Extraordinary deprivations of liberty: disappearances

The European Court of Human Rights has reviewed a number of cases raising claims of violations of Article 5 in connection with the disappearances of persons last seen in the custody or control of the governmental authorities, including military or security forces. Where credible evidence exists that an individual has in fact disappeared in such circumstances, the Court will normally reject any arguments of the State that it has no documentation showing that the individual has ever been in its custody or control. For example, in the case of *Kurt v. Turkey* (1998) the Court reviewed a complaint that the authorities had failed to account for the whereabouts or fate of the applicant's son who had last been seen surrounded by members of the security forces. In finding a violation of Article 5, the Court stressed that the purpose of the guarantees afforded by that Article, and particularly the requirements of promptitude and judicial control guaranteed under Articles 5(3) and 5(4), was to minimise the risk of arbitrariness by making the act of deprivation of liberty amenable to independent judicial scrutiny as well as securing governmental accountability for that deprivation. The Court also noted that such prompt judicial intervention was an important means to detect and prevent life-threatening measures or serious ill-treatment. In the instant case, the authorities had kept no records related to the initial detention of the person or his subsequent whereabouts or fate. The Court found that the failure to keep data recording such matters as the date, time and location of detention, the name of the detainee as well as the reasons for the detention and the name of the person effecting it were incompatible with the purpose of Article 5.

The Court has applied the above principles in a long series of cases relating to disappearances of individuals whilst in governmental custody or control. In *Kurt*, as well as in other similar cases, the Court has also reviewed the seriousness with which the authorities have conducted investigations into the disappearances. In this context, it should be noted that the same principles apply to investigations and accountability under Article 5 as under Articles 2 and 3, including the principle that no statute of limitations should apply to the obligation to conduct an effective investigation into alleged disappearances. For example, in the case of *Cyprus v. Turkey* (2001), the Court found a continuing violation of Article 5 where the Turkish authorities failed to conduct an investigation into the whereabouts and fate of Greek Cypriot missing persons in respect of whom there was an arguable claim that they were in Turkish custody at the time of their disappearance decades previously.

4. Procedural protections guaranteed under Article 5

With the exception of Article 5(3), which provides specific protections only to individuals deprived of their liberty in accordance with Article 5(1)(c), the procedural protections afforded under Article 5 are guaranteed in the context of deprivations of liberty in both the civil and the criminal context. Protection against arbitrary deprivations of liberty is the principle underlying these procedural protections. In this respect, discrepancies between domestic law and practice may be the sole factor leading to the finding of a violation of Article 5. However, in some instances the Court has found that minor defects in procedures governing detention in the civil context are not sufficient grounds to support the finding of a violation of Article 5 (*Winterwerp v. the Netherlands* (1979), *Rutten v. the Netherlands* (2001) and *Douiyeb v. the Netherlands* (1999)).

Right to be informed of charges: Article 5(2)

Article 5(2), which sets forth the right of an individual to be informed promptly, in a language he or she understands, of the reasons for his or her arrest and any charges against him or her, does not demand that the information provided be as detailed as that prescribed under Article 6(3) with respect to criminal charges. The Court has found a violation of Article 5(2) only once, in the case of *Van der Leer v. the Netherlands* (1990). In this case, the Dutch authorities failed to supply the applicant not only with information about the grounds for her detention in a psychiatric hospital, but also failed to inform her that she was in fact being deprived of her liberty. In contrast, if it is clear that an individual being detained is aware of the reasons for his or her detention, there will be no violation of Article 5(2) (*Čonka v. Belgium* (2002) (authorities had summoned individuals to complete papers necessary for the completion of asylum requests and subsequently deported them) and *Dikme v. Turkey* (2000) (applicant himself had noted that certain accusations had been made against him during his initial interrogation by the Security Police)).

Procedural protections in connection with pre-trial detention: Article 5(3)

The provision of Article 5(3) which requires that persons detained under Article 5(1)(c) must be brought promptly before a judge or other judicial officer encompasses both procedural and substantive protection for such persons. The Court has held that compliance with Article 5(3) requires the judicial authority to review all issues relating to the detention question, and take the final decision by reference to objective legal criteria. In order to fulfil this role, the authority before which the individual in question must be brought must hear what he or she has to say. It must then take its decision independently and in accordance with procedures and norms established by law (*Schiesser v. Switzerland* (1979)).

The judicial authority determining the necessity of an initial period of detention must be empowered to order the release of an individual should it decide that such detention is not necessary (*Aquilina v. Malta* (1999) and *Sabeur Ben Ali v. Malta* (2000)). Such an authority must also both have the power and take the initiative to consider the possibility of granting bail in lieu of detaining someone (Aquilina). In this context, it is worth noting that a decision to grant bail *ipso facto* constitutes a decision that the individual concerned would pose no risk to society or to the proper conduct of the proceedings. It follows that detaining the individual while details of his or her bail are finalised may violate Article 5(3), as occurred in the case of *Iwańczuk v. Poland* (2001).

With respect to the independence and impartiality of the judicial officer, the Court has held that for a state official to exercise the role of both prosecutor and investigator does not meet these requirements (*Skoogström v. Sweden* (1984) and *Huber v. Switzerland* (1990)). Nor is it acceptable for a detention decision to be taken by a prosecutor (*Niedbala v. Poland* (2000)) or by an investigator whose decisions are subject to control by the prosecuting authorities (*Assenov v. Bulgaria* (1998) and *Nikolova v. Bulgaria* (1999)). In the context of deprivations of liberty within the military, Article 5(3) does not permit a commanding officer to take such a decision, where that commanding officer will have an adjudicative role to play in connection with related court martial proceedings (*Hood v. the United Kingdom* (1999) and *Stephen Jordan v. the United Kingdom* (2000)).

The term "promptly" in Article 5(3) represents a more stringent standard than does the term "speedily" in Article 5(4). Although the case-law does not prescribe a firm minimum standard, it is clear that incommunicado detention for periods of from twelve to fourteen days, without the detained individuals having been brought before a competent judicial authority, constitutes a violation of Article 5(3) (*Aksoy v. Turkey* (1996) and *Sakik and Others v. Turkey* (1997)). The Court has not accepted governmental arguments that similar periods of incommunicado detention could be justified by the existence of a state of emergency in the region in these cases or subsequent cases from the same region (see, for example, *Demir and Others v. Turkey* (1998) and *Dikme v. Turkey* (2000)). Similarly, in the cases of *Brogan and Others v. the United Kingdom* (1988) and *O'Hara v. the United Kingdom* (2001), the Court held that four days and six hours and six days and thirteen hours respectively were too long periods to meet the standard, in spite of the special difficulties attached to investigating terrorist offences.

The Court has accepted as initial grounds for detention such factors as likelihood of flight from the jurisdiction (*Neumeister v. Austria* (1968), *Stögmüller v. Austria* (1969) and *Matznetter v. Austria* (1969)), and the risk of the committal of further offences (*Matznetter*). However, the Court has made it clear that Article 5(3) is not intended to permit a State to detain an individual indefinitely. Continued detention may be justified in a given case only if there are clear indications of a genuine public interest which, notwithstanding the presumption of innocence, outweighs the right to liberty, if the national judicial authorities examine the circumstances for or against the existence of such an imperative interest and set them out in their decisions on the applications for release. The persistence of a reasonable suspicion that the person arrested has committed an offence is a condition sine qua non for the lawfulness of the continued detention, but the Court has noted that after a certain lapse of time it no longer suffices and judicial authorities must advance other grounds that are both "relevant" and "sufficient" to justify the continued deprivation of liberty (*Punzelt v. the Czech Republic* (2000)). Whatever grounds may exist to justify continued detention, the State must also conduct the proceedings with special diligence (*Letellier v. France* (1991), *Van der Tang v. Spain* (1995), *Assenov and Others v. Bulgaria* (1998) and *Punzelt v. the Czech Republic* (2000)).

Article 5(3) also guarantees the right to trial within a reasonable time if an individual has not been released. The notion of "reasonable time" under Article 5(3) covers the period from moment of arrest to judgment at the first instance. The Court found a violation of this provision where an individual was held in pre-trial detention for four years, although he had voluntarily admitted having committed the offences at issue at the beginning of the investigation (*Muller v. France* (1997)). It found fifteen months unreasonable in a case in which the domestic authorities had provided no reasons to justify the continuation of the applicant's detention on remand and in light of a domestic legal provision to the effect that any time during which an individual had access to his or her case file did not count as part of the period of detention (*Ječius v. Lithuania* (2000)). Although an accused person in detention is entitled to have his or her case given a higher priority than that of someone who is at liberty, the interim release of an accused person from detention does not nullify the right to trial within a reasonable time (*Wemhoff v. Germany* (1968)).

Habeas corpus/Amparo: Article 5(4)

Article 5(4) provides an individual deprived of his or her liberty through arrest or detention the right to challenge in court the lawfulness of such deprivation. Such a challenge must be heard by a judicial body that is independent and impartial in proceedings whose fairness is guaranteed by a range of procedural safeguards. A challenge to the lawfulness of a deprivation of liberty must be heard speedily, and the individual must be released if the court decides that a given detention is unlawful. Unlike Article 5(3), which applies to the initial phase of detention of an individual suspected of involvement in a criminal offence, Article 5(4) applies on an ongoing basis to deprivations of liberty effected in either the civil or the criminal context.

Many individuals raising claims of violations of Article 5(4) have alleged that the authorities have failed to conduct regular periodic reviews of the legality of their deprivations of liberty. Through these cases, the Court has established the general principle that the introduction of new issues or the change of circumstances of a given detainee may necessitate a new assessment of the need to continue to deprive him or her of liberty, even though the original detention decision was legitimate. This principle is particularly well-developed in cases in which individuals have been deprived of their liberty on the grounds of mental disorders or psychiatric disturbances, regarding which the Court has held that such individuals are entitled to review of the legality of detention at reasonable intervals (see, for example, *Winterwerp v. the Netherlands* (1979)). In cases in which individuals have been deprived of their liberty as a result of a criminal conviction, the Court has also held that once the punishment phase of a criminal sentence has been served, an individual is entitled to regular review of any period of detention imposed thereafter (*Oldham v. the United Kingdom* (2000), *Stafford v. the United Kingdom* (2002), *Hussain v. the United Kingdom* (1996), *Singh v. the United Kingdom* (1996) and *Curley v. the United Kingdom* (2000)).

The "lawfulness" of a deprivation of liberty

Article 5(4) guarantees must be provided for in the domestic law of all High Contracting Parties (*Sabeur Ben Ali v. Malta* (2000) (no remedy in Maltese law for challenging lawfulness of detention); *Ječius v. Lithuania* (2000) and *Grauslys v. Lithuania* (2000) (existence of a statutory bar to appeal against court decisions authorising detentions)). The available remedy must be effective and sufficiently certain (i.e. there must be review of the *legality* of the detention itself, not just procedures or abuses of power). Note that Article 5(4) requires the States Parties to the Convention to provide a domestic remedy, the effectiveness of which the Court may review in light of standards developed also under other Articles of the Convention. In the case of *Sakik and Others v. Turkey* (1997), the Court found a violation of this provision in part on the grounds that the government could show no examples where an individual had successfully invoked either Article 5(4) or the cognate Article of the Turkish Constitution.

The Court has made clear that Article 5(4) calls for a judicial determination of the continuing lawfulness of detention, finding violations in cases in which executive authorities have been afforded excessive discretion in this regard (see, for example, *Stafford v. the United Kingdom* (2002), *T. v. the United Kingdom* (1999) and *V. v. the United Kingdom* (1999)).

Where the authorities place obstacles in the way of individuals wishing to seise the judicial body competent to review the lawfulness of their detention, the Court will find a violation of Article 5(4) (*Čonka v. Belgium* (2002) (applicants summoned to complete asylum requests, arrested and expelled within a time frame that rendered it impossible to obtain judicial review)).

The nature of a court and the fairness of proceedings under Article 5(4)

The judicial body reviewing claims related to deprivations of liberty must be independent and impartial and guarantee procedural safeguards of a judicial character (for example, access to court, legal representation in some instances, and sufficient information about the grounds for detention to be able to mount an effective challenge). Principles of fairness must be met even if the State invokes national security concerns as a ground for detaining a particular individual (*Chahal v. the United Kingdom* (1996)).

Consistent with its holdings also with respect to Article 5(3), where executive authorities are empowered to determine detention issues without their decisions being amenable to judicial review, the Court will find a violation of Article 5(4) (*Kampanis v. Greece* (1995), *Nikolova v. Bulgaria* (1999), *Kawka v. Poland* (2001) and *Dougoz v. Greece* (2001)). In the context of psychiatric detention, the Court has found a violation of Article 5(4) where a judge had examined the applicant previously, expressed his opinion about her condition outside the court and then participated in the decision-making process, noting that although the protections afforded by Article 5(4) were not as stringent as those afforded by Article 6(1), impartiality was not a standard that could be so compromised (*D.N. v. Switzerland* (2001)).

The Court has held that the equality of arms principle applies in habeas corpus proceedings: there must be an adversarial procedure (*Sanchez-Reisse v. Switzerland* (1986) and *Wloch v. Poland* (2000)). In this light, an accused must have access to the files used by the investigating authorities in their review of a decision to detain the accused on remand (*Lamy v. Belgium* (1989)) and must be provided with any submissions in this regard made by the prosecuting authorities (*Niedbala v. Poland* (2000)). In the case of a person whose detention falls within the ambit of Article 5(1)(c), a hearing is required (*Graužinis v. Lithuania* (2000) and *Trzaska v. Poland* (2000)).

Furthermore, a detainee may be entitled to legal representation in Article 5(4) proceedings where arguments for or against detention require a certain expertise or legal sophistication (*Sanchez-Reisse v. Switzerland* (1986)) or where a very young person has been detained (*Bouamar v. Belgium* (1988)). In the event that a detainee has legal representation, that representation must be effective and impartial (*Magalhães Pereira v. Portugal* (2002) (court-appointed lawyer failed to play a role in detention proceedings, leading court to appoint an official from the detention facility to represent the applicant) and, in particular, cannot be obstructed by the government (*Lietzow v. Germany* (2001) (applicant's lawyer had no access to the criminal files in connection with review of his detention on remand) and *Kawka v. Poland* (2001) (applicant and his lawyer were not entitled to be informed about grounds for detention or to participate in proceedings in which the prosecutor was fully involved).

A judicial body reviewing the lawfulness of detention cannot place an onerous burden on the individual, for example, by demanding that the individual bear the burden of proof to demonstrate that he or she would not abscond, re-offend or obstruct justice (*Nikolova v. Bulgaria* (1999)).

Speedy review under Article 5(4)

Whether the Court will consider a State to have taken a decision on the lawfulness of detention "speedily", as required by Article 5(4), will depend on a number of factors, including the nature of the detention at issue. In *Bezicheri v. Italy* (1989), for example, the Court clarified that the intervals for review of decisions to detain on remand must be relatively short, whereas the intervals for review in psychiatric detention cases might be somewhat longer without running afoul of the Convention. In this instance, an interval of five and a half months for examination of a second application for release from detention on remand was too long. In the case of *De Jong, Baljet and Van den Brink v. the Netherlands* (1984), the Court found that a delay of between six and eleven days was too long to wait for an initial review of a detention decision. It has also found violations with respect to delays of twenty-two days (*Rehbock v. Slovenia* (2000)), thirty-four days and thirty-three days (*M.B. v. Switzerland* (2000)), between three and six months (*Baranowski v. Poland* (2000)) and three to seven months (*Ilowiecki v. Poland* (2001)).

In cases dealing with review of psychiatric detention decisions, the Court has found violations with respect to delays of four months (*Koendjbiharie v. the Netherlands* (1990)), eight weeks (*E. v. Norway* (1990)), one year, eight months and nine days (*Musial v. Poland* (1999)) and two and a half years (*Magalhães Pereira v. Portugal* (2002)).

5. Right to compensation under Article 5(5)

Article 5(5) sets forth an enforceable right to compensation for "everyone who has been the victim of arrest or detention in contravention of the provisions of [... Article 5]". In order for the Court to find a violation of Article 5(5), it must first find a violation of one or more of the rights protected by the preceding paragraphs of the Article (*Murray v. the United Kingdom* (1994)). It is important to note that the right to compensation under this provision is a right an individual claims from national authorities. In order to be in compliance with Article 5(5), a State must establish a basis in domestic law for compensation where there has been a breach of any of the rights guaranteed under Article 5, whether through incorporation of the Convention in domestic law or other means (see, for example, *Curley v. the United Kingdom* (2000) and *D.G. v. Ireland* (2002)).

In the above-mentioned *Sakik* case, the Court found a violation of Article 5(5) on the grounds that the Turkish Government could not show that anyone had ever been compensated under the domestic legal provisions the Government cited as applicable. In the case of *Tsirlis and Kouloumpas v. Greece* (1997), the Court also found a violation of Article 5(5) where the applicants had been detained in contravention of domestic law and thus of Article 5(1) as well, and where the domestic courts refused to compensate them for their unlawful detention on the specious grounds that they had been detained as a result of their own gross negligence.

As discussed elsewhere, Article 41 of the Convention confers on the European Court of Human Rights the competence to "afford just satisfaction" to an individual in certain circumstances (see Chapter 21 below). The Court has held that these two provisions do not operate on a mutually exclusive basis and that the disposition of a claim under Article 5(5) does not preclude the possibility of Court review of the matter under Article 41 (*Brogan and Others v. the United Kingdom* (1988) and *Ciulla v. Italy* (1989)).

6. Freedom of movement: Article 2 of Protocol No. 4

Article 2 of Protocol No. 4 provides for two substantive rights: that everyone lawfully within the territory of a State shall have the right to liberty of move-ment and freedom to choose his or her residence, and that everyone shall be free to leave any country. The Article also provides for two types of restric-tions on the rights: general limitations like those set forth in the second para-graphs of Articles 8 to 11 of the Convention itself, and the specific limitation that a State may restrict the rights of liberty of movement and freedom to choose a residence when justified "by the public interest in a democratic society". Note that a State may not invoke "the public interest" in order to prevent someone from emigrating, an important point for countries expe-riencing "brain drain" or other serious losses of human resources. The Court has found violations of this provision where a State has imposed a series of restrictions on an individual's freedom of movement, including obligations to report regularly and frequently to the police (*Raimondo v. Italy* (1994)) or to remain at one's place of residence during the course of bankruptcy pro-ceedings, when those proceedings took a number of years (*Luordo v. Italy* (2003) (over fourteen years) and *Bottaro v. Italy* (2003) (twelve years and six months)).

Chapter 6 – The right to a fair hearing: Article 6 and Articles 2 to 4 of Protocol No. 7

Convention – Article 6

1.   In the determination of his civil rights and obligations or of any criminal charge against him, everyone is entitled to a fair and public hearing within a reasonable time by an independent and impartial tribunal established by law. Judgment shall be pronounced publicly but the press and public may be excluded in the interest of morals, public order or national security in a democratic society, where the interests of juveniles or the protection of the private life of the parties so require, or to the extent strictly necessary in the opinion of the court in special circumstances where publicity would prejudice the interests of justice.

2.   Everyone charged with a criminal offence shall be presumed innocent until proved guilty according to law.

3.   Everyone charged with a criminal offence has the following minimum rights:

    a.   to be informed promptly, in a language which he understands and in detail, of the nature and cause of the accusation against him;

    b.   to have adequate time and facilities for the preparation of his defence;

    c.   to defend himself in person or through legal assistance of his own choosing or, if he has not sufficient means to pay for legal assistance, to be given it free when the interests of justice so require;

    d.   to examine or have examined witnesses against him and to obtain the attendance and examination of witnesses on his behalf under the same conditions as witnesses against him;

    e.   to have the free assistance of an interpreter if he cannot understand or speak the language used in court.

Protocol No. 7 – Article 2

1.   Everyone convicted of a criminal offence by a tribunal shall have the right to have his conviction or sentence reviewed by a higher tribunal. The exercise of this right, including the grounds on which it may be exercised, shall be governed by law.

2.   This right may be subject to exceptions in regard to offences of a minor character, as prescribed by law, or in cases in which the person concerned was tried in the first instance by the highest tribunal or was convicted following an appeal against acquittal.

Protocol No. 7 – Article 3

When a person has by a final decision been convicted of a criminal offence and when subsequently his conviction has been reversed, or he has been pardoned, on the ground that a new or newly discovered fact shows conclusively that there has been a miscarriage of justice, the person who has suffered punishment as a result of such conviction shall be compensated according to the law or the practice of the State concerned, unless it is proved that the non-disclosure of the unknown fact in time is wholly or partly attributable to him.

Protocol No. 7 – Article 4

No one shall be liable to be tried or punished again in criminal proceedings under the jurisdiction of the same State for an offence for which he has already been finally acquitted or convicted in accordance with the law and penal procedure of that State.

The provisions of the preceding paragraph shall not prevent the reopening of the case in accordance with the law and penal procedure of the State concerned, if there is evidence of new or newly discovered facts, or if there has been a fundamental defect in the previous proceedings, which could affect the outcome of the case.

No derogation from this Article shall be made under Article 15 of the Convention.

Article 6 of the Convention guarantees the right to a fair and public hearing in the determination of an individual's civil rights and obligations or of any criminal charge against him. The Convention organs interpret Article 6 broadly, on the grounds that it is of fundamental importance to the operation of democracy. The first paragraph of Article 6 applies to both civil and criminal proceedings, whereas the second and third paragraphs apply exclusively to criminal cases.

1. What are "civil rights and obligations"?

The Court interprets the notion of "civil rights and obligations" quite broadly. In the *Ringeisen v. Austria case* (1971), the Court held that Article 6(1) covers all proceedings the result of which is decisive for private rights and obligations, whatever the character of either the legislation that governs how a matter is to be determined or the authority exercising jurisdiction in the matter. Where a right is set forth in the domestic law of a State, the Court will most often consider it a civil right in the sense of Article 6(1) (see, for example, *Balmer-Schafroth and Others v. Switzerland* (1997) (the right to have physical integrity protected), *Winterwerp v. the Netherlands* (1979) and *Matter v. Slovakia* (1999) (determination of status of having civil capacity), and (*Tolstoy Miloslavsky v. the United Kingdom* (1995) and *Kurzac v. Poland* (2001) (the right to enjoy honour and a good reputation)).

In order for Article 6 to apply in the civil context, a "dispute" over a civil right must exist. The Court has held on several occasions that Article 6(1) applies to proceedings whose outcome has a direct bearing on the determination and/or substantive content of a private right or obligation (*König v. Germany* (1978) (withdrawal of right to run a private medical clinic and to continue to exercise the medical profession); *Le Compte, Van Leuven and De Meyere v. Belgium* (1981) (disciplinary proceedings before professional association); *De Moor v. Belgium* (1994) (establishing right to be admitted to the Bar); *Feldbrugge v. the Netherlands* (1986) (proceedings brought in order to continue receiving a health insurance allowance); *Deumeland v. Germany* (1986) (proceedings brought in order to obtain a widow's supplementary pension) and *Schouten and Meldrum v. the Netherlands* (1994) (contesting obligations to make contributions to social security schemes)). Proceedings before constitutional courts are also governed by Article 6, where the outcome of such proceedings will be decisive for a civil right protected by that Article (*H. v. France* (1989) and *Kraska v. Switzerland* (1993)).

Even abstract review of a law may be decisive for the enjoyment of a civil right and thus covered by requirements of fairness (*Süssmann v. Germany* (1996)). In fact, any proceeding whose outcome is decisive for the determination of a civil right must meet the requirements of Article 6 (*Ringeisen v. Austria* (1971)). Decisions taken by constitutional courts on the merits of a given case may be considered "determinations" in the sense of Article 6, but such a court's decision on the conformity of decisions taken by domestic tribunals with constitutional law may not (*Sramek v. Austria* (1984) and *Buchholz v. Germany* (1981)).

2. What is meant by "criminal charge"?

As with respect to the notion of a "civil right or obligation", the European Court of Human Rights takes a broad view of the notion of a "criminal charge" under Article 6 of the Convention, applying three criteria to determine whether a particular matter falls within its purview: the domestic legal classification of the offence, the nature of the offence and the nature and severity of the possible penalty (*Pierre-Bloch v. France* (1997)). The Court has held that a State cannot remove an offence from the protection of Article 6 simply by declaring the offence to be "non-punishable" (*Adolf v. Austria* (1982) and *Öztürk v. Germany* (1984)). Where large tax surcharges are imposed as a result of tax audits, the Court has found that the general character of the relevant legal provisions on tax surcharges, the deterrent and punitive purposes of the penalties and the severity of the potential and actual penalty brought the matter within the scope of a "criminal charge" under Article 6 (*Janosevic v. Sweden* (2002) and *Västberga Taxi Aktiebolag and Vulic v. Sweden* (2002)).

With respect to when a person is considered to be "charged" with a criminal offence in the sense of Article 6(1), the Court has held that this transpires at the point when the State takes "measures which carry the implication of ... an allegation [that he or she has committed a criminal offence] and which likewise substantially affect the situation of the suspect" (*Foti and Others v. Italy* (1982)). The Convention institutions have found the "substantial effect" standard to be met by such actions as the publication of a warrant or the search of premises or persons. On the other hand, they have not found the standard to be met by the launching of a police investigation, the questioning of witnesses, or other activities without direct effect on the individual.

The sentencing phase of a criminal proceeding is also governed by Article 6. The Court thus found a violation of Article 6 where the Secretary of State rather than the court fixed the tariff period for a convicted prisoner (*V. v. the United Kingdom* (1999) and *Easterbrook v. the United Kingdom* (2003)).

3. What are not "civil rights and obligations" or "criminal charges"?

Article 6 applies where there is an arguable "protected interest", for example, almost any right set forth in domestic law, or accrued rights such as pension rights, where contributions have been made to a pension fund. It does not apply to public law matters, such as decisions regarding the entry, stay and deportation of aliens (*Maaouia v. France* (2000)), extradition (*Mamatkutlov and Abdurasulovic v. Turkey* (2004)) or electoral disputes (*Pierre-Bloch v. France* (1997)). As noted above, Article 6 does not apply where there is no dispute at law (*Kienast v. Austria* (2003)).

The obligation to pay taxes normally falls outside the scope of Article 6, as the Court considers that tax matters form part of the core of public-authority prerogatives (*Ferrazzini v. Italy* (2001)). However, if authorities may impose fines or other penalties by way of a criminal sanction with respect to taxation disputes, Article 6 will apply under its criminal head (*Västberga Taxi Aktiebolag and Vulic v. Sweden* (2002) and *Janosevic v. Sweden* (2002)). The Court also draws the same distinction with respect to the exercise of the prerogative powers of a court to ensure the orderly conduct of proceedings through the imposition of sanctions for disorderly conduct by one of the parties (*Putz v. Austria* (1996)). In both contexts, the Court will consider such factors as the deterrent or punitive purpose of any sanction imposed, as well as its nature and severity, to determine if a matter falls within the purview of the criminal head of Article 6(1).

In general, Article 6 does not apply to internal relations between governmental agencies and their employees (*Neigel v. France* (1997) (proceedings for reinstatement after a period of leave); nor will it apply where the employee exercises a portion of the State's sovereign powers (*Pellegrin v. France* (1999) and *Mosticchio v. Italy* (2000)). However, where an individual exercises only a low level of responsibilities in the public sector, the Court has held that Article 6 may apply (see, for example, *Frydlender v. France* (2000) (failure to renew contract as a technical adviser to the government) and *Devlin v. the United Kingdom* (2001) (alleged discrimination in recruitment for a low level position in the civil service)).

Article 6 may not apply to measures that are not very severe and are of a temporary nature, even in the criminal context (*Escoubet v. Belgium* (1999) (temporary withdrawal of a driving licence following accident); *Janosevic v.*

Sweden (2002) and *Västberga Taxi Aktiebolag and Vulic v. Sweden* (2002) (courts refused to stay execution of enforcement measures pending long-delayed appeals of tax assessors' decisions)). However, where the effect of a temporary measure is severe and may have irreversible effects on the outcome of proceedings for the determination of a right, Article 6 will be applicable (*Markass Care Hire Ltd. v. Cyprus* (2001) (interim decision of court that applicant company was to hand over a large portion of its rental fleet to a company with which it had a rental agreement)).

4. The right to a court under Article 6(1)

The fair administration of justice begins with the guarantee that an individual has access to a court that provides all the attributes of a judicial form of review. Access to a judicial forum must be substantive, not just formal. Any restriction placed on access to a court or tribunal must pursue a legitimate aim and the means employed must be proportionate to that aim (*Tinnelly & Sons Ltd. and Others and McElduff and Others v. the United Kingdom* (1998)). Although access to court may be limited in some circumstances, for example through the operation of statutory limitation periods, requiring a litigant in a civil suit to provide security for legal costs when lodging an appeal, or limiting the standing of minors or persons of unsound mind, any such limitation cannot be such as to impair the essence of the right to a court (*Brualla Gómez de la Torre v. Spain* (1997), *Tolstoy Miloslavsky v. the United Kingdom* (1995), *Kreuz v. Poland* (2001) and *Aït-Mouhoub v. France* (1998)). The Court may find a violation of Article 6 should an appellate court strike out an appeal on the grounds that the appellant has failed to implement fully the judgment appealed against (*Annoni di Gussola and Others v. France* (2000), *Bayle v. France* (2003), *Pages v. France* (2003) and *García Manibardo v. Spain* (2000)).

In some circumstances, professional legal assistance is necessary to ensure that an individual enjoys the right to a court. For indigent persons, this requirement may be fulfilled by the granting of legal aid (*Airey v. Ireland* (1979) and *Aerts v. Belgium* (1998)), or, in the event that no civil legal aid scheme exists, through alternative means (*Andronicou and Constantinou v. Cyprus* (1997)). Should a legal aid board determine that professional assistance is crucial to the proper conduct of a case, the right to effective access to court demands that such representation be provided (*Bertuzzi v. France* (2003) (refusal of successive lawyers to represent legally aided applicant in bringing damages action against another lawyer). However, the Court has also found that a State may refuse to grant legal aid without falling foul of Article 6 where it is clear that the individual requesting such legal aid is well-versed in the applicable law and has not been confronted with complex issues (*McVicar v. the United Kingdom* (2002)) or where no serious grounds for appeal exist that require expert legal assistance (*Del Sol v. France* (2002) and *Essaadi v. France* (2002)).

A State cannot restrict or eliminate judicial review of disputes that fall within the scope of Article 6(1) (*Glod v. Romania* (2003) (lawfulness of decisions of an administrative body) and *Popovici and Dumitrescu v. Romania* (2003) (nationalisation of property)), or with respect to certain categories of individuals (*Golder v. the United Kingdom* (1975) (prisoners), *Keegan v. Ireland* (1994), *Sommerfeld v. Germany* (2001) and *Hoffmann v. Germany* (2001) (unmarried fathers), *Luordo v. Italy* (2003) (bankrupts), *Philis v. Greece* (1991) (engineer practising independently), *Canea Catholic Church v. Greece* (1997) and *The Holy Monasteries v. Greece* (1994) (selected churches and monasteries)). Nor can a State act to affect the outcome of proceedings pending before the courts or to limit the effects of certain judgments through the operation of law (*Stran Greek Refineries and Stratis Andreadis v. Greece* (1994), *Papageorgiou v. Greece* (1997), *Multiplex v. Croatia* (2003), *Kutić v. Croatia* (2002), *Zielinski and Pradal and Gonzalez and Others v. France* (1999), *Anagnostopoulos and Others v. Greece* (2000)). Even in the absence of legislation affecting the outcome of judicial proceedings, in the event that a court declines to review facts crucial to the determination of a dispute, thereby depriving itself of its own jurisdiction, there will be a violation of the right of access to court (*Terra Woningen B.V. v. the Netherlands* (1996), *Chevrol v. France* (2003), *Rotaru v. Romania* (2000) and *Koskinas v. Greece* (2002)), as there will be in the event that a court asks a ministry to interpret a treaty and subsequently dismisses a claim based on that interpretation (*Beaumartin v. France* (1994)). Finally, executive authorities charged with the enforcement of a valid court judgment cannot refuse to do so (*Jasiūnienė v. Lithuania* (2003), *Antonakopoulos, Vortsela and Antonakopulou v. Greece* (1999) (refusal of authorities to implement final and binding court judgments)).

Possibility of *ex post facto* interference by executive authorities

The principle of the rule of law entails a duty on the part of the state or other public authority to comply not only with judicial orders or decisions against it, but also with decisions taken in the context of administrative proceedings (*Hornsby v. Greece* (1997) and *Immobiliare Saffi v. Italy* (1999)).

Where executive authorities have the unilateral power to request the revision or nullification of final court judgments, there may be a violation of Article 6. For example, where several governmental authorities are empowered to lodge objections to the outcome of court proceedings, the Court held that the risk that final court decisions could repeatedly be set aside was *ipso facto* incompatible with the principle of legal certainty (*Sovtransavto Holding v. Ukraine* (2002)). The violation may arise also where the highest judicial authority ascribes responsibility for handling complaints about violations of protected rights to executive authorities, as occurred in the cases of *Vasilescu v. Romania* (1998) and *Brumărescu v. Romania* (1999).

In some instances, executive authorities responsible for the enforcement of judicial decisions have taken their own decisions to obstruct or to delay indefinitely such enforcement. In the case of *Satka and Others v. Greece* (2003), the State deprived judgments regarding the ownership of property of any practical effect by issuing a series of administrative decrees dictating how the property was to be used, and in the case of *Immobiliare Saffi v. Italy* (1999) and numerous parallel cases, the prefectures charged with enforcing court judgments ordering the return of residential property had exercised their discretion to stagger the granting of police assistance to effect the judicially ordered evictions. A State may not invoke financial difficulties experienced by the State to justify its failure to pay compensation awarded by a court (*Burdov v. Russia* (2002)).

Access to court and immunity

Although Article 6 applies to many disputes between an individual and a State, various immunities of States or State agents or employees may bar courts from adjudicating such cases. International organisations may be granted immunity from civil suits in the domestic courts of their host countries (*Waite and Kennedy v. Germany* (1999) (employment dispute)). Similarly, the immunity enjoyed by diplomatic missions and embassies may pose a procedural bar on the power of domestic courts to review certain civil complaints (*Fogarty v. the United Kingdom* (2001) (employment recruitment dispute)). With respect to civil disputes outside the area of employment law, the Court found no violation of Article 6 where the United Kingdom courts had held that the Kuwaiti Government was immune from civil suit in the United Kingdom for damages for personal injury suffered under torture by Kuwaiti governmental agents (*Al-Adsani v. the United Kingdom* (2001)). Again, in *McElhinney v. Ireland* (2001), the Court found that Ireland could afford immunity to the United Kingdom with respect to the actions of British soldiers in Northern Ireland to the extent that torts committed by them could be considered as *acta jure imperii.* In finding that Ireland had not exceeded its margin of appreciation in limiting the right of access to a court, the Court noted that the applicant could have pursued his complaint through the British courts.

A State that grants itself or its employees immunity from civil liability on the grounds of "public interest immunity" must nevertheless provide other means for individuals who have suffered injuries as a result of State action or conduct to obtain redress for those injuries (*Osman v. the United Kingdom* (1998)). Similarly, granting members of the judiciary immunity from civil liability will be compatible with Article 6 if alternative means exist for an individual to pursue a remedy for any damage suffered as a result of action taken by a member of the judiciary (*Ernst and Others v. Belgium* (2003)). The Court has found that it was not permissible for a member of a parliament to avoid prosecution for defamation where the contested dispute arose outside the context of political matters, where the immunity of the individual was derived from a resolution passed by the parliament itself and where no other means was open to the individual to have the alleged defamation redressed (*Cordova v. Italy* (*Nos. 1 and 2*) (2003)).

5. Other aspects of Article 6(1)

As noted above, Article 6(1) refers to both civil and criminal proceedings, whereas Articles 6(2) and 6(3) apply to criminal matters only. It is important to keep in mind, therefore, that the general requirements of Article 6(1) permeate the requirements of the more specifically focused Articles. There also exist underlying principles of "fairness" that are not articulated in the Article itself but are important to understanding its operation.

Independence and impartiality of tribunals: general points

The principles underlying the independence and impartiality of a tribunal are closely allied to those governing the right to a court (see above section). The principle underlying the independence and impartiality clause of Article 6(1) is the separation of powers, but neither the Convention itself nor the Convention organs dictate the means by which this requirement should be met. However, it is clear from the case-law that neither the legislative nor the executive branch of government should interfere with the operation of the judiciary. It thus found a violation in the case of *Sovtransavto Holding v. Ukraine* (2002) where the President of Ukraine had written to the Supreme Arbitration Tribunal, asking it to "defend the interests of Ukrainian nationals" against those of the Russian applicant company. Where judicial and legislative functions are combined, there will also be a violation (*McGonnell v. the United Kingdom* (2000) (Guernsey bailiff presided over judicial proceedings contesting application of Development Plan over which he presided in the legislature as Deputy Bailiff)).

As discussed above with respect to the right to a court, governmental authorities may neither fail nor refuse to implement decisions taken by judicial tribunals (*Hornsby v. Greece* (1997)).

With respect to the independence and impartiality of a tribunal itself, the Court has established that even if individuals are technically qualified to address a given issue and even if there is no subjective reason to doubt their personal integrity, it is important that the appearance of objective impartiality and independence is preserved (*Langborger v. Sweden* (1989)). Primarily, this standard requires that those adjudicating a particular matter cannot be seen to have a relationship with any of the parties (*Sramek v. Austria* (1984) (member of a court was subordinate in terms of his professional duties to one of the parties), *Pescador Valero v. Spain* (2003) (judge was employed part-time by a party to the proceedings) and *Sigurdsson v. Iceland* (2003) (husband of judge indebted to one of the parties)).

Judicial authorities who have been involved in initial stages of proceedings against an individual may not participate in the adjudication of criminal charges against him or her (*Tierce and Others v. San Marino* (2000), *Rojas Morales v. Italy* (2000), *Castillo Algar v. Spain* (1998)). Nor may a judge in a position of authority within the court system appoint judges to hear a case in which he or she has an interest (*Daktaras v. Lithuania* (2000)).

In the case of *De Cubber v. Belgium* (1984), it was not acceptable for the investigating judge and the trial judge to be the same person, and in the *Piersack v. Belgium* case (1982), the same result obtained where the president of the tribunal had earlier been the public prosecutor on the case being adjudicated. In the case of *Hauschildt v. Denmark* (1989), the Court found a violation of Article 6 where the trial judge had previously ruled on the detention on remand of the accused, on the ground that decisions on detention must take into account indicia of guilt and thus could prejudice the objectivity of the trial.

The Convention does not require trial by jury. However, where a country has instituted a jury system, the requirements of independence and impartiality apply. The Court found a violation where a majority of members of the jury had links with the defendant in the case (*Holm v. Sweden* (1993) and where members of a jury had allegedly made racist remarks against a minority group of which a defendant was a member (*Sander v. the United Kingdom* (2000)).

Independence and impartiality of tribunals: courts martial and national security courts

The Court has reviewed a number of cases complaining about the independence and impartiality of national security courts, courts martial or other tribunals operating in a military or quasi-military context. The European Court of Human Rights has established a strong line of cases prohibiting the trials of civilians by military tribunals, particularly where there are close structural links between the executive authorities and the military officers conducting such trials (see, for example, *Çiraklar v. Turkey* (1998) and *Incal v. Turkey* (1998)).

With respect to courts martial, issues arise with respect to the supervision or control of the process by non-judicial authorities. For example, in the case of *Findlay v. the United Kingdom* (1997), the Court found a violation of Article 6 where the "convening officer" at the court martial had remanded the applicant for trial, appointed members of the court martial panel, appointed the prosecuting and defending officers and confirmed the sentence imposed. Everyone with a role in the court martial was subordinate in rank to the convening officer and fell within his chain of command. Although certain reforms were subsequently introduced in the court martial system, the Court nevertheless still found flaws in the case of *Morris v. the United Kingdom* (2002), where two young judges had been appointed to a court martial panel on an ad hoc basis and the only channel of final appeal against a negative decision was to a non-judicial "reviewing authority", to which leave to appeal had been refused by the court martial appeal court without a hearing. However, the Court found no violation of Article 6 where the president of a court martial panel was on his last posting prior to retirement, and thus not subject to evaluation by his superior officers, and where the two ordinary members had received training in disciplinary procedures (*Cooper v. the United Kingdom* (2003)).

The establishment of a tribunal "by law"

The Court has found a violation of the requirement that a tribunal be established by law in only a few cases. In the case of *Coëme and Others v. Belgium* (2000), the Court found a violation of this provision where the Court of Cassation connected private persons to criminal proceedings against a government minister. In connecting these cases, the Court referred to a general constitutional provision according it jurisdiction over criminal cases against government ministers, but made no reference to any legal basis for it to try private persons. Where the law itself dictates the composition of a court, non-compliance with the terms of that law will lead to the finding of a violation of the requirement that a tribunal be established by law (*Posokhov v. Russia* (2003) and *Lavents v. Latvia* (2002)).

The right to trial "within a reasonable time"

By far the largest number of cases reviewed by the European Court of Human Rights have alleged violations of the right to a fair trial within a reasonable time. The factors which the Convention institutions have established for the evaluation of whether a given proceeding has met the "reasonable time" standard are the complexity of a given case, the conduct of the authorities, the conduct of the applicant, and what is at stake for the applicant (see, for example, *Buchholz v. Germany* (1981)).

The Court evaluates the complexity of a case in light of such factors as the nature of the facts or legal questions at issue, the number of actors involved as defendants, parties or witnesses, the conduct of parallel or related proceedings and any international elements.

With respect to the conduct of the applicant, the Court has held that an individual charged with a criminal offence is under no obligation to assist in the acceleration of proceedings against him or her (*Eckle v. Germany* (1982)). The conduct of an individual's legal counsel is attributable to him or her, and thus when delays are caused primarily by the actions of counsel, the Court will find no violation of Article 6 (*Punzelt v. the Czech Republic* (2000)).

With respect to the conduct of the authorities, the Court considers that the State is responsible for all delays caused by any administrative or judicial authority. It is incumbent on the States to organise their legal systems in order to ensure that trials can be held within a reasonable time. The Court has rejected governmental arguments that inadequate staffing or general administrative inconvenience are sufficient justifications for failure to meet the "reasonable time" standard (*De Cubber v. Belgium* (1984) and *Guincho v. Portugal* (1984)). Nor has the Court been sympathetic to governmental arguments that political circumstances can justify lengthy delays, where those circumstances arose years after the introduction of proceedings (*Pammel v. Germany* (1997) and *Probstmeier v. Germany* (1997)). A temporary backlog of business does not involve liability on the part of the Contracting States provided that they take prompt remedial action to deal with an exceptional situation.

The time in civil proceedings runs from the date the proceedings begin and in criminal proceedings from the date of the charge. In civil proceedings, the time is calculated to include not only the time it takes to reach a final decision in a case, but also the time it takes for the enforcement of the judgment (*Di Pede v. Italy* (1996) and *Guillemin v. France* (1997)). In the context of criminal cases, the Court has established that the time runs from the time "official notification [has been] given to an individual by the competent authority of an allegation that he has committed a criminal offence" (*Deweer v. Belgium* (1980)). In the case of *Eckle v. Germany* (1982), the Court added "the test whether 'the situation of the [suspect] has been substantially affected'", the same standard that applies in determining whether one should be considered to have been charged with a criminal offence. (In the Eckle case, the two sets of proceedings had continued for seventeen and ten years respectively.) The period for consideration ends when the decision of the highest instance domestic body becomes final.

In general the Court will allow a State more leeway with respect to the length of civil proceedings than criminal ones. It has consistently held to a strict standard in cases contesting the length of compensation proceedings brought by individuals infected with HIV through contaminated blood supplies (*X v. France* (1992), *Karakaya v. France* (1994) and *A. and Others v. Denmark* (1996)) and with respect to proceedings concerning the taking of children into public care and related matters (*Hokkanen v. Finland* (1994) and *Ignaccolo-Zenide v. Romania* (2000)).

When considering what is at stake for the applicant in connection with complaints about the length of proceedings, the European Court of Human Rights will take cognisance of other protected rights that may be negatively affected by unduly long proceedings (*Strategies and Communications and Dumoulin v. Belgium* (2002) (business interests harmed by length of criminal investigation into managing director, including retention by the authorities of essential accounting documents)). In this regard, it has noted that proceedings for the determination of child custody or access must be held with particular alacrity (see, for example, *Nuutinen v. Finland* (2000) and *E.P. v. Italy* (1999)), as must proceedings to determine an individual's legal capacity based on mental health grounds (*Matter v. Slovakia* (1999) and *Lutz v. France* (*No. 2*) (2003)).

Although in principle the Court can only review matters arising after the entry into force of the Convention for a particular High Contracting Party, in cases raising complaints about the length of proceedings under Article 6, the Court will also take into consideration the situation prevailing at that point.

The right to a public hearing

The object of publicity of judicial proceedings is to protect individuals against the secret administration of justice. The interests to be served by public proceedings are not only those of the parties, but those of the public at large: to ensure confidence in the administration of justice. It follows that a proceeding that is open only to the parties and their representatives does not meet the requirements of this provision of the Convention (*Kadubec v. Slovakia* (1998) and *Malhous v. the Czech Republic* (2001)). Nor is the requirement of publicity met when a criminal trial is held within a prison, unless measures are taken to ensure that the public is informed about the location of the prison, access requirements and similar matters (*Riepan v. Austria* (2000)). However, the press and public may be excluded from disciplinary hearings held within prisons (*Campbell and Fell v. the United Kingdom* (1984)). The publicity requirement applies to any phase of a proceeding which affects the "determination" of the matter at issue (*Axen v. Germany* (1983)).

The Court has clarified that the public hearing requirement normally encompasses also the right to an oral hearing (*Ezelin v. France* (1991), *Bakker v. Austria* (2003), *Stefanelli v. San Marino* (2000), *Forcellini v. San Marino* (2003) and *Sigurthor Arnarsson v. Iceland* (2003)), particularly where a party to the case specifically requests one (*Fischer v. Austria* (1995) and *Eisenstecken v. Austria* (2000)) or where only one judicial instance reviews the facts and law (*Fredin v. Sweden (No. 2)* (1994) and *Fischer v. Austria* (1995)). However, the Court has held that a hearing may not be necessary in a case that raises issues of fact and law that can be adequately resolved on the basis of the case file and the written submissions of the parties. In all circumstances, however, judgments must be pronounced publicly (*Rushiti v. Austria* (2000)).

6. Fairness of proceedings: additional aspects

As noted above, the Court has elucidated the principles of fairness through a wide range of cases, many of which raise complex issues. The key consideration of the Court in its review of such cases is whether the proceedings as a whole can be considered to meet the standards of fairness in the sense of Article 6(1) of the Convention.

The equality of arms principle

The most important of the unarticulated principles of Article 6 is the "equality of arms" – the idea that each party to a proceeding should have equal opportunity to present his case (*Neumeister v. Austria* (1968)), and that neither should enjoy any substantial advantage over his opponent. The equality of arms principle encompasses the notion that both parties to a proceeding are entitled to have information about the facts and arguments of the opposing party and that each party must have an equal opportunity to reply to the other. The Court has found violations of this principle where a domestic court based its judgment on submissions about which one of the parties had no knowledge (*Slimane-Kaïd v. France* (2000), *MacGee v. France* (2003), *Krčmář and Others v. the Czech Republic* (2000), *Fortum Corporation v. Finland* (2003), *APEH Üldözötteinek Szövetsége and Others v. Hungary* (2000) and *Walston v. Norway* (2003)); where one side was denied access to relevant documents contained in the case file (*Kerojärvi v. Finland* (1995), *McMichael v. the United Kingdom* (1995) and *Foucher v. France* (1997)) or was refused the right to have certain evidence considered (*De Haes and Gijsels v. Belgium* (1997) and *Mantovanelli v. France* (1997)), including that of expert witnesses (*Bönisch v. Austria* (1985)); where courts considered submissions from only one party (*Hiro Balani v. Spain* (1994), *Ruiz Torija v. Spain* (1994), *Van Orshoven v. Belgium* (1997), *Quadrelli v. Italy* (2000) and *Keegan v. Ireland* (1994)); and where a party was not informed about relevant dates in proceedings against him (*Vacher v. France* (1996), *K.D.B. v. the Netherlands* (1998) and *Fretté v. France* (2002)). Prosecuting authorities are under an affirmative obligation to disclose evidence of value to the defence in a timely and effective way (*Kuopila v. Finland* (2000) and *Dowsett v. the United Kingdom* (2003)). The presence of a governmental representative during the deliberations of a court may lead to the exercise of undue influence over the proceedings (*APBP v. France* (2002)).

In the cases of *Colozza v. Italy* (1985), *Monnell and Morris v. the United Kingdom* (1987), *Botten v. Norway* (1996) and *Lobo Machado v. Portugal* (1996) the Court further held that in most circumstances defendants must be present and entitled to take part in any proceedings.

In cases involving the removal of children from their parents, termination of parental rights and similar issues going to the fundamental basis of the right to family life, the Court has found violations in circumstances in which a child has been removed from its mother within hours of birth and made available for adoption one week later, without the parents having been provided with the opportunity to obtain legal counsel and without the competent judicial authority having raised important issues (*P., C. and S. v. the United Kingdom* (2002)). Similar circumstances have arisen in other cases involving young children (see, for example, *Buchberger v. Austria* (2001) and *T.P. and K.M. v. the United Kingdom* (2001)).

In cases involving juveniles, different considerations may apply with respect to the equality of arms principle than will apply in cases involving adults. For example, the Court found a violation of Article 6 where two young children accused of murder were found to be suffering from post-traumatic stress disorder and to have only very limited ability to instruct their lawyers, testify adequately in their own defence or otherwise participate fully in the proceedings, which were themselves both highly publicised and public (*V. v. the United Kingdom* (1999) and *T. v. the United Kingdom* (1999)).

Good faith compliance with procedural rules

Needless to say, should a domestic court make a procedural error that affects the fairness of a proceeding and thereafter fail to rectify it, there will be a violation of Article 6 (*Leoni v. Italy* (2000)). The Court has also found violations of Article 6 where domestic tribunals have applied formal procedural rules too rigidly (*Pérez de Rada Cavanilles v. Spain* (1998) and *Miragall Escolano and Others v. Spain* (2000)), in instances in which they have reneged on representations made to a litigant (*Sovtransavto Holding v. Ukraine* (2002) (court invited applicant to lodge an appeal to repair a formal defect and then dismissed the appeal on the grounds that the deadline had passed), and where a court has refused to review essential evidence or to consider the substance of a claim raised (*Tinnelly & Sons Ltd. and Others and McElduff and Others v. the United Kingdom* (1998)). Should the possibility of pursuing civil claims depend on the successful prosecution of a related criminal offence, any failure of the authorities to pursue the requisite prosecution may constitute a violation of Article 6 (*Anagnostopooulos v. Greece* (2003)).

A lack of clarity in procedural rules that govern particular proceedings may lead the Court to find a violation of Article 6(1) on the grounds of fairness. It did so in the case of *Coëme and Others v. Belgium* (2000), where a government minister was tried by the Court of Cassation without having been apprised of the procedural rules that would apply prior to the start of the trial, and in the case of *Vacher v. France* (1996), where the Court of Cassation dismissed an appeal on points of law for the failure of the applicant to lodge a pleading on the matter, without informing him of the time limit for filing such a pleading.

Reasoned judgments

Article 6(1) obliges courts to give reasons for their decisions. In particular, lower courts or other decision-making authorities must give adequate reasons to enable parties to make effective use of any existing right of appeal (*H. v. Belgium* (1987)). Assuming that this requirement has been met, an appellate court may, in principle, simply endorse the reasons for the lower court's decision (*García Ruiz v. Spain* (1999) and *Helle v. Finland* (1997)).

A Court may not substitute its own reasoning for that of medical experts in determining the necessity for a particular type of treatment or surgery (*Van Kück v. Germany* (2003)). Nor will it be compatible with Article 6 for a decision making body to provide internally contradictory reasoning (*Hirvisaari v. Finland* (2001) (body supported a reduction in a disabled individual's pension on the grounds that his condition had deteriorated since the grant of a full pension)).

Trials *in absentia*

An individual who has absented himself or herself from proceedings governed by Article 6 does not thereby forfeit the protections afforded. The Court has held that a domestic court may neither refuse to allow legal counsel to represent an absent client (*Van Geyseghem v. Belgium* (1999), *Van Pelt v. France* (2000) and *Pobornikoff v. Austria* (2000)), nor dismiss an appeal on points of law on the same grounds (*Guérin v. France* (1998), *Omar v. France* (1998), *Khalfaoui v. France* (1999), and *Papon v. France* (2002)).

Although the Court has not prohibited the conduct of trials *in absentia* in cases in which the defendant is untraceable, it has consistently held that anyone convicted in such a trial will be entitled to a new trial on his or her return to the jurisdiction (*Colozza v. Italy* (1985) and *Osu v. Italy* (2002)).

Should an individual who has been released on bail subject to an obligation to appear for trial then abscond from the jurisdiction and subsequently be tried *in absentia,* he or she may not complain about a lack of access to court (*Karatas and Sari v. France* (2002)).

The privilege against self-incrimination

The Court has reviewed several cases in which an individual has claimed a violation of his or her right not to incriminate himself or herself, a principle not explicitly included in the Convention. The main factor the Court reviews in such cases is whether the totality of the circumstances related to the alleged self-incrimination could be considered to be coercive. The Court has found that such coercive circumstances obtain where an employee of a company is compelled to make statements or provide information about business activities to governmental authorities investigating possible improprieties and the information so obtained is adduced in subsequent criminal proceedings against that employee (*Saunders v. the United Kingdom* (1996) and *I.J.L. and Others v. the United Kingdom* (2000)). It has also done so where an individual was fined for his refusal to produce bank statements and legal papers that customs authorities believed to exist but could not find during the course of a legal search of his premises (*Funke v. France* (1993)).

In a line of cases arising in connection with the conduct of police interrogations, the Court has found violations of Article 6 where central use was made at trial of incriminating statements an individual had provided to police whilst being kept incommunicado in oppressive detention conditions and without access to a solicitor (*Magee v. the United Kingdom* (2000)). It has also done so even without considering the use made in court of statements or evidence obtained through questionable methods (*Heaney and McGuinness v. Ireland* (2000) (applicants provided with conflicting information about their rights during the course of police interrogations that effectively extinguished their right to remain silent)). Similarly, the Court has occasionally reviewed complaints about the use of undercover agents in connection with criminal investigations. It found no violation of the right to a fair proceeding in the case of *Lüdi v. Switzerland* (1992), as the police officer concerned had been sworn in, the investigating judge was aware of his mission and the authorities had opened a preliminary investigation of the applicant. However, it came to the opposite conclusion in the case of *Teixera de Castro v. Portugal* (1998), where the police acted independently of any judicial supervision, the applicant had no previous criminal record and no preliminary investigation had been opened against him.

Related to the use of incriminating statements gained through coercion is the issue of adverse inferences being drawn from an individual's exercising his or her right to remain silent, an important aspect of the privilege against self-incrimination. The Court has found violations of both Article 6(1) and Article 6(2) (guaranteeing the right to be presumed innocent) where individuals have been convicted for refusing to answer police questions (*Heaney and McGuinness v. Ireland* (2000) and *Quinn v. Ireland* (2000)). Even where an individual has not faced penal sanctions for refusing to answer questions, the Court will find a violation where police have provided conflicting or unclear advice about the scope of the right to remain silent, particularly where an individual has not had access to legal counsel (*Averill v. the United Kingdom* (2000)). The Court has also found that inadequate instructions to a jury about the nature of inferences that could be drawn from the silence of an individual in the face of police questioning constitute a violation of Article 6, as defects in such instructions could not be repaired on appeal (*Condron v. the United Kingdom* (2000) (applicant had been detained and questioned whilst suffering from heroin withdrawal symptoms)).

7. The presumption of innocence: Article 6(2)

Article 6(2) enshrines in the Convention the right to be presumed innocent. The underlying principle of this right is that an individual charged with a criminal offence is entitled to the benefit of the doubt (the *in dubio pro reo* principle).The European Court of Human Rights has reviewed cases dealing with three aspects of this right. With respect to the first aspect, that the onus of adducing sufficient evidence to prove guilt falls on the prosecution, the Court has found a violation in only a few cases. In *Telfner v. Austria* (2001), it did so where domestic courts had convicted the applicant based on very weak evidence and speculation about his involvement in an automobile accident. It also did so where a State imposed punitive fines on the heirs to the estates of individuals who had been found guilty of tax evasion, holding that criminal liability could not be transferred to innocent parties (*A.P., M.P. and T.P. v. Switzerland* (1997) and *E.L., R.L. and J.O. -L. v. Switzerland* (1997)).

With respect to the second aspect, that governmental authorities or the media are prohibited from making public statements about the guilt of an individual prior to the final determination of the criminal charge, the Court has found violations of Article 6(2) where the chairman of the parliament publicly declared guilty a government minister who had been charged with a criminal offence (*Butkevičius v. Lithuania* (2002)) and where a governmental official and the policeman in charge of a criminal investigation declared a suspect guilty prior to any charges having been filed against him (*Allenet de Ribemont v. France* (1995)).

With respect to the third aspect, that post-trial proceedings cannot be used as a forum for implying the criminal guilt of an individual who has been acquitted, or against whom charges have been dropped, the Court has found violations where such an individual has been assessed for court costs or financial penalties in circumstances that implied guilt (*Minelli v. Switzerland* (1983) (case dropped due to the running of the statute of limitations)). The Court has also found violations of Article 6(2) where domestic courts have refused to award compensation for time spent in detention to individuals who had been acquitted, on the grounds that suspicions remain that the individuals were guilty of the offences (*Sekanina v. Austria* (1993), *Rushiti v. Austria* (2000), *Lamanna v. Austria* (2001) and *Weixelbraun v. Austria* (2001)) or where they have held that the balance of probabilities showed that the acquitted individuals had committed the acts in question (*O. v. Norway* (2003) and *Hammern v. Norway* (2003)).

However, the Court found no violation of Article 6(2) where an award of compensation in civil proceedings was made against a person previously acquitted of criminal offences concerning the same facts (*Ringvold v. Norway* (2003)). In *Phillips v. the United Kingdom* (2001) the Court held that Article 6(2) was not applicable to confiscation proceedings conducted after conviction, as part of the sentencing process.

8. Procedural protections under Article 6(3)

As with the presumption of innocence of paragraph 2, the protections afforded by paragraph 3 supplement the right to a fair hearing of paragraph 1. The converse also applies with regard to paragraph 3, however, as it outlines some of the *minimum* rights to be afforded to a criminal defendant, not the totality of the protection guaranteed by Article 6 (*Adolf v. Austria* (1982)). The evaluation of fairness in general is, therefore, always open to review.

The right to be informed promptly, in a language he understands, in detail: Article 6(3)(a)

To date, there has been little case-law under this provision of Article 6(3). In the case of *Brozicek v. Italy* (1989), the Court found a violation of the right to be informed where a resident of one country was charged with a criminal offence in another country and was served with papers to that effect in the language of the second country which proceeded to try him *in absentia* and ultimately to find him guilty, without ever responding to his request for translations of the relevant papers. In the case of *Kamasinski v. Austria* (1989), the Court held that the State's provision of a defence counsel capable of communicating in both the language of the court and the language of the applicant fulfilled the requirements of Article 6(3)(a).

More recently, the Court has reviewed complaints about the quality of information provided in formal criminal charges, finding violations where an appeal court reclassified a criminal charge and failed to provide the defence with an opportunity to prepare and submit additional arguments (*Pélissier and Sassi v. France* (1999)), where criminal charges were not precise (*Mattoccia v. Italy* (2000) (finding also violations of 6(1) and 6(3)(b)) and where the authorities imposed a fine on an individual for abuse of process without a hearing (*T. v. Austria* (2000) (finding also a violation of 6(3)(b)).

The right to adequate time and facilities for the preparation of his defence: Article 6(3)(b)

This provision is closely connected with the right to be fully informed about criminal charges, guaranteed by Article 6(3)(a), and the right to legal representation guaranteed by Article 6(3)(c). The Court has found violations of this provision where a court has recharacterised a criminal offence at a stage of criminal proceedings when it is no longer possible for the defendant to react (*Sadak and Others v. Turkey* (2001) and *Mattoccia v. Italy* (2000)) or where witnesses change their testimony during the course of proceedings and the defence is not provided with an adequate opportunity to challenge them (*G.B. v. France* (2001)).

The Court has stressed that one of the most important "facilities" for the preparation of a defence against criminal charges is adequate opportunity to consult with legal counsel (*Campbell and Fell v. the United Kingdom* (1984)). Where investigative authorities only permit such consultations to take place under their surveillance there will be a violation (*Lanz v. Austria* (2002)), as there may be even where the authorities have delayed in sending a letter from a prisoner to his lawyer (*Domenichini v. Italy* (1996)).

Consistent with the notion of the "determination" of a charge discussed above, the "adequate time and facilities" requirement of Article 6(3)(b) extends to appellate proceedings. The Court thus found a violation of this provision in conjunction with Article 6(1) where a military court provided inadequate reasoning in its judgment and permitted only a short period of time to file an appeal (*Hadjianastassiou v. Greece* (1992)).

The right to defend himself or through legal assistance of his own choosing/legal aid: Article 6(3)(c)

Article 6(3)(c) ties the right to defence and, where necessary, the provision of free legal assistance to the requirements of "the interests of justice", which to a great extent correspond to respect for the principle of equality of arms discussed above. The Court has held that the right to be given legal assistance for free when the interests of justice so require is not an alternative to the right to defend oneself, but an independent right to which objective standards apply. Criteria for determining whether the interests of justice require that an individual be provided with free legal assistance include the nature of the charges against the applicant and the need to develop arguments on complicated legal issues (*Pham Hoang v. France* (1992) and *Twalib v. Greece* (1998)).

In principle, if an individual may be deprived of his or her liberty, the interests of justice require legal representation (*Quaranta v. Switzerland* (1991), *Benham v. the United Kingdom* (1996) and *Perks and Others v. the United Kingdom* (1999)). Even if an individual is already serving a criminal sentence, he or she retains the right to counsel in connection with any criminal charges brought against him or her whilst in prison (*Ezeh and Connors v. the United Kingdom* (2003)). Should the State grant free legal assistance to an individual charged with a criminal offence, it cannot then withdraw that assistance before the final determination of the charge at the highest instance (*R.D. v. Poland* (2001)).

If a given case raises legal issues that require the application of a certain level of professional expertise, the State cannot demand that an accused attempt to address such issues himself (*Pakelli v. Germany* (1983) and *Artico v. Italy* (1980)). In the case of *Granger v. the United Kingdom* (1990), the applicant had been refused legal aid to cover the costs of legal representation at an oral appellate hearing against a conviction for perjury: the domestic appeals court had itself adjourned the hearing in order to consider a complex point of law on the merits of the claim. The Court found the State in violation of Articles 6(1) and 6(3)(c) taken together. Although the United Kingdom Government made certain changes in practice as a result of this decision, they were found insufficient in the cases of *Boner v. the United Kingdom* (1994) and *Maxwell v. the United Kingdom* (1994).

In a number of cases raising issues under Article 6(3)(c), the Court has emphasised the distinction between de jure and de facto protection. For example, the Court has found violations of this provision where court-appointed defence counsel have failed to act diligently on behalf of their clients (*Artico v. Italy* (1980), *Goddi v. Italy* (1984) and *Daud v. Portugal* (1998)). Consistent with the idea that the assistance of counsel must be effective, the Court has also found violations of Article 6(3)(c) where a court dismissed an appeal at a hearing at which defence counsel was absent, having not been informed about the date (*Alimena v. Italy* (1991) and in several cases in which courts refused to permit counsel to represent clients who were not themselves in attendance at the hearings (*Poitrimol v. France* (1993), *Lala v. the Netherlands* (1994), *Pelladoah v. the Netherlands* (1994), *Van Geyseghem v. Belgium* (1999), *Van Pelt v. France* (2000) and *Karatas and Sari v. France* (2002)). Finally, the Court has held that defence counsel and defendant must be able to communicate freely and with full respect for the confidentiality of their communications, whether written or oral (*S. v. Switzerland* (1991)) (see also discussion of Article 6(3)(b) above). They also must be able to do so in a timely way at the time of arrest or detention in circumstances in which the rights of the defence might otherwise be irretrievably prejudiced (*John Murray v. the United Kingdom* (1996) (adverse inferences could ultimately be drawn against the applicant should he remain silent during initial police interrogations)).

With respect to the right to choose one's counsel, the Court has held that States are entitled to institute specialised Bars or to limit the number of lawyers entitled to appear before particular courts without falling foul of Article 6 of the Convention (*Reinhardt and Slimane-Kaïd v. France* (1998) and *Meftah and Others v. France* (2002)).

The right to confront witnesses: Article 6(3)(d)

The wording and the case-law of Article 6(3)(d) support the principle of equality of arms which underlies Article 6 in its entirety. For example, in the case of *Bönisch v. Austria* (1985), the Court held that a trial court must follow that same pattern of interrogation in examining its own expert witnesses and those called by the defence. The right to call or confront witnesses is not an unlimited right. Courts may determine the number of witnesses a party may call or the necessity of hearing a particular witness in order to establish the facts of the case or otherwise contribute to a fair adjudication (*Perna v. Italy* (2003) (no violation of Article 6(1) and 6(3)(d) for not calling a witness whose testimony would consist of a denial of allegations against him)). However, in the event that a court refuses to admit evidence proposed by a party, it must provide reasons for the refusal (*Pisano v. Italy* (2000) and *Suominen v. Finland* (2003)).

A defendant must be given an adequate and proper opportunity to challenge and question a witness against him or her either when the witness makes initial statements or at a later stage of the proceedings (*Isgrò v. Italy* (1991) and *Lucà v. Italy* (2001)). This opportunity must be afforded to a defendant even if it is difficult to gain access to a particular witness, for example when he or she lives outside the jurisdiction (*A.M. v. Italy* (1999)).

The Court has often found violations of Article 6(3)(d) where convictions have been based on the testimony of anonymous witnesses unavailable for questioning by the defence (*Kostovski v. the Netherlands* (1989), *Windisch v. Austria* (1990), *Saïdi v. France* (1993) and *Birutis and Others v. Lithuania* (2002)). It has also found violations where the witnesses were police officers, whether anonymous (*Van Mechelen v. the Netherlands* (1997)), or identified but made unavailable for the purposes of confrontation (*Hulki Güneş v. Turkey* (2003)).

Some cases have raised issues relating to the granting to certain witnesses of "privileged" status by operation of given domestic laws. In the event that the testimony of a witness concerned forms an important foundation for the case, the Court will find a violation should the defence be unable to confront that witness (*Unterpertinger v. Austria* (1986), *Bricmont v. Belgium* (1989) and *Sadak and Others v. Turkey* (2001)).

The right to free interpretation: Article 6(3)(e)

The Court has given a broad interpretation of the right to free assistance of an interpreter where an accused does not understand the language used in court. In the case of *Luedicke, Belkacem and Koç v. Germany* (1978), the Court stated that this provision applies to "all those documents or statements in the proceedings... which it is necessary for him to understand in order to have the benefit of a fair trial". It elaborated on this requirement, listing among the items demanding interpretation or translation at the expense of the authorities the charge, the reasons for arrest, and the hearing itself. In theory, the case-law establishes that an accused himself or herself must understand virtually all aspects of his or her case. However, in the case of *Kamasinski v. Austria* (1989), the Court found no violation of Article 6(3)(e) where the defence counsel was formally competent in the mother tongue of the accused.

9. Rights guaranteed under Protocol No. 7

Relatively few cases have arisen under Protocol No. 7 to the Convention. However, the Court found a violation of Article 2 of Protocol No. 7 in the case of *Krombach v. France* (2001). In this case, a man who had been tried and convicted *in absentia* by an assize court was prohibited by law from appealing against his conviction or from contesting the validity of certain procedural actions to the competent second instance court. The European Court of Human Rights considered that the restriction on the rights guaranteed under this provision infringed the essence of the right, particularly given that he wished to challenge the refusal of the assize court to allow his legal counsel to represent him in the first instance proceedings. The Court also found violations of Article 4 of Protocol No. 7 in only a few cases, in each of which the applicant had been found guilty of both an administrative and a criminal offence on the basis of the same facts (*Gradinger v. Austria* (1995), *Franz Fischer v. Austria* (2001), *W.F. v. Austria* (2002) and *Sailer v. Austria* (2002)).

Chapter 7 – Freedom from retroactive criminal legislation: Article 7

Article 7

1.   No one shall be held guilty of any criminal offence on account of any act or omission which did not constitute a criminal offence under national or international law at the time when it was committed. Nor shall a heavier penalty be imposed than the one that was applicable at the time the criminal offence was committed.

2.   This Article shall not prejudice the trial and punishment of any person for any act or omission which, at the time when it was committed, was criminal according to the general principles of law recognised by civilised nations.

Throughout the case-law of the European Court of Human Rights, "lawfulness" in the sense of the Convention is considered as comprising three general elements: accessibility, foreseeability and protection against the arbitrary actions of governmental authorities. Article 7 ties these principles to a specific context: the application of material criminal law.

Article 7(1) of the Convention protects an individual from being convicted for a criminal offence which did not exist in law at the time the act was committed. This reflects the principle that only the law can define a crime and prescribe a penalty (*nullum crimen, nulla peona sine lege*). It follows that one must have notice of a prohibited form of conduct in order to be held responsible for its infringement.

The applicants in the cases of *Streletz, Kessler and Krenz v. Germany* (2001) and *K.–H.W. v. Germany* (2001) had been convicted of intentional homicide in connection with the killings of individuals who had attempted to cross the border between the German Democratic Republic (GDR) and the then Federal Republic of Germany (FRG). Three of the applicants had been convicted in their capacity as indirect principals, by virtue of their participation in the decision-making processes at senior levels of the GDR government in the institution of the border policing policy calling for the use of lethal force against anyone attempting to cross the border. The fourth applicant had been convicted for killing named individuals who had attempted to do so. The Court noted that the applicants, who had held very senior positions in the GDR government, could be presumed not only to have been fully cognisant of both the applicable domestic law but to have been instrumental to its implementation. The Court further noted that the applicant who had shot those attempting to cross the border could not defend his actions on the grounds of blindly obeying orders. Throughout, the Court emphasised that the domestic law in force in the GDR at the material time clearly delineated the criminal offences for which the applicants had been convicted. Given the clarity and accessibility of the applicable law, the Court found that the criminal convictions of the applicants did not contravene Article 7(1) of the Convention.

In instances in which claims have been raised that an individual was convicted of a criminal offence under an unclear legal provision, the Court has taken a common sense approach, holding that the development of rules of criminal liability through judicial interpretation may constitute such notice, where that development is consistent with the essence of the offence at issue and could reasonably be foreseen. In the cases of *C.R. v. the United Kingdom* (1995) and *S.W. v. the United Kingdom* (1995), the Court held that criminal convictions for attempted rape of one's wife and rape of one's wife did not violate Article 7 of the Convention, and stated:

> [T]he abandonment of the unacceptable idea of a husband being immune against prosecution for rape of his wife was in conformity not only with a civilised concept of marriage but also, and above all, with the fundamental objectives of the Convention, the very essence of which is respect for human dignity and human freedom.

The Court has also held that an individual actively engaged in a profession normally exercises caution in pursuing his or her occupation and may reasonably be expected to take legal advice in this regard where a relevant law might be open to differing interpretations and where criminal liability may ensue for its breach. In the event that an individual has reason to understand and to assess the risks involved in pursuing a particular course of action, the imposition of criminal liability does not lead to a violation of Article 7 (*Cantoni v. France* (1996)).

The Court has held that where the elements of a criminal offence are changed, such changes cannot be applied retroactively to the detriment of an individual charged with the offence at issue. In the case of *Veeber v. Estonia* (2003), the material criminal law at the time of the alleged commission of the offence required the existence of a previous administrative punishment for a similar offence as a pre-condition for a criminal conviction. No such punishment had been applied with respect to the applicant. The Court found a violation of Article 7 on the grounds that the applicant could not have foreseen that he would risk a criminal conviction under the circumstances.

Article 7(1) further prohibits a State from imposing on an individual convicted of a criminal offence a more severe penalty than the one that applied at the time of the commission of the offence. The Court has clarified that the notion of a penalty in the sense of Article 7 is a broad one, potentially covering any detriment to which the individual was exposed at the time of the commission of the offence. The Court has found violations of this provision where more severe penalties have been imposed on individuals convicted of criminal offences than were applicable at the time the offences were committed (*Ecer and Zeyrek v. Turkey* (2001)) as well as in cases where individuals have been sentenced to prison terms under laws that did not provide for this penalty for the individuals concerned (*E.K. v. Turkey* (2002) (book editor sentenced under a statute that only allowed such a penalty for periodical and newspaper editors)) and *Başkaya and Okçuoğlu v. Turkey* (1999) (book publisher sentenced under a statute that only allowed such a penalty for book editors)). In the case of *Welch v. the United Kingdom* (1995), the Court held that the confiscation of the applicant's property under a statute passed after his conviction for a crime for which the new law provided such a penalty constituted a violation of Article 7.

The Court also found violations of Article 7(1) in cases in which individuals had been sentenced to serve longer sentences than were permitted under the domestic law (*Jamil v. France* (1995) (State prolonged a prison sentence by twenty months where the maximum permissible sentence at the time he committed the original crime was four months) and *Gabarri Moreno v. Spain* (2003) (domestic courts had recognised an error in the sentence imposed but failed to rectify it)).

The scope of Article 7 is limited primarily to substantive criminal law. It follows that the Court did not find a violation of Article 7 in a case in which the applicants complained about changes to the statute of limitations and related procedural rules governing criminal prosecutions (*Coëme and Others v. Belgium* (2000) (the nature of the criminal offences at issue remained unchanged)) or in a case in which the applicant complained that the competent authorities had rejected several applications for the remission of his sentence (*Grava v. Italy* (2003) (remission of a sentence relates to the execution of the sentence and not to the imposition of the sentence itself)).

Article 7(2) excludes from the prohibition against retroactive law any acts which were considered to be criminal at the time they were committed "according to the general principles of law recognised by civilised nations". This provision clearly harks back to the Nuremburg (and Tokyo) Principles and their focus on war crimes. The wording itself, however, is lifted directly from Article 38 of the Statute of the International Court of Justice. It is worth noting in this context that the use of the term "civilised nations" implies that the law and practice of States beyond the universe of the High Contracting Parties to the European Convention on Human Rights must be taken into consideration when applying Article 7(2). As of the end of 2003, the Court had not reviewed any case claiming a breach of this provision.

Chapter 8 – Grounds for restricting the exercise of rights under the Convention: paragraphs 2 of Articles 8 to 11 and Article 2 of Protocol No. 4/ Article 17/ Article 18

(NOTE: For the text of the second paragraphs of Article 8, 9, 10, or 11, or Article 2 of Protocol No. 4, please refer to the chapters discussing the substantive rights protected by these Articles.)

Articles 8, 9, 10, and 11 of the Convention itself and Article 2 of Protocol No. 4 share a similar structure. The first paragraphs of these Articles guarantee certain specific rights and freedoms, whereas the second paragraphs of the same Articles (or in the case of Article 2 of Protocol No. 4, the third paragraph) set forth both general guidelines and specific grounds a High Contracting Party may invoke to restrict the operation of those rights and freedoms. This structure serves to help balance the rights of the individual and the broader interests of the democratic society as a whole in instances where they may be in conflict (*Klass and Others v. Germany* (1978)).

In the event that the Court finds that there has been no interference with the exercise or enjoyment of a right protected under the first paragraph of the relevant Article, it may stop its examination of the claim at issue at that point. However, even in the absence of such an interference, the Court may still consider whether a State has failed to meet any positive obligation necessary to secure the right or freedom.

1. Doctrine of inherent limitations

One of the important issues the Convention institutions have had to address in cases where the balance between the individual and the society has been raised is whether the grounds permitting restrictions listed in the various Articles should be considered to be exhaustive, or whether a State should be permitted to impose restrictions on certain types of individuals on "implied" or policy grounds. Early on in the life of the Convention, the Court rejected the argument that rights could be so restricted, holding that although a State could consider a person's status as a member of a particular group as one factor to be taken into account when restricting his or her rights or freedoms, it nevertheless could only legitimately act within the confines of the specific limitations clauses of the relevant Articles of the Convention (*De Wilde, Ooms and Versyp ("Vagrancy") v. Belgium* (1970, 1971, 1972); *Golder v. the United Kingdom* (1975)).

2. Rule of strict interpretation of limitations clauses

The restrictions clauses contained in the second paragraphs noted above are themselves quite broad. In order to ensure that States Parties do not abuse the power inherent in this breadth, the Convention institutions established a rule of strict interpretation for these clauses, stating in the case of *Sunday Times v. the United Kingdom* (1979):

> Strict interpretation means that no other criteria than those mentioned in the exception clause itself may be at the basis of any restrictions, and these criteria, in turn, must be understood in such a way that the language is not extended beyond its ordinary meaning.

The rule of strict interpretation applies both to the two general conditions common to all the qualifying paragraphs under discussion, that any restrictions on rights and freedoms must be lawful and "necessary in a democratic society", and to the more specific grounds listed in the separate Articles. When reviewing a case in which the government has invoked one or more of the restrictive clauses of the Article in question, the Court pursues the following line of analysis. First, it will determine whether or not the State action was "in accordance with law". If it finds that it was not, the Court will find a violation and will not proceed with further review (see, for example, *Rotaru v. Romania* (2000)). If it finds that the action met the legality standard, it will then examine whether that action could be considered "necessary in a democratic society" for one of the legitimate purposes listed in the relevant Article, such as the preservation of public order, the protection of health or morals, and so forth.

3. The interpretation of the phrase "in accordance with law/prescribed by law"

The concept of legality under the Convention applies to all types of domestic laws – administrative, statutory, and constitutional, written and unwritten (*Golder v. the United Kingdom* (1975), *Silver and Others v. the United Kingdom* (1983), and *Sunday Times v. the United Kingdom* (1979)). The Court has established two major requirements of lawfulness, as set forth in the *Sunday Times* case:

> Firstly, the law must be adequately accessible: the citizen must be able to have an indication that is adequate in the circumstances of the legal rules in a given case. Secondly, a norm cannot be regarded as a "law" unless it is formulated with sufficient precision to enable the citizen to regulate his conduct....

Thus, in order for a particular State action or enactment to be considered to be "in accordance with law" under the Convention, it must be both *accessible* and *foreseeable*. The Court further developed the notion of legality in the case of *Malone v. the United Kingdom* (1984), by tying it to the prohibition against State abuses of power:

> It would be contrary to the rule of law for the legal discretion granted to the executive to be expressed in terms of an unfettered power. Consequently, the law

must indicate the scope of any such discretion conferred on the competent authorities and the manner of its exercise with sufficient clarity, having regard to the legitimate aim of the measure in question, to give the individual adequate protection against arbitrary interference.

Thus, the third element comprising legality under the Convention is the existence of guidelines and mechanisms through which the exercise of State discretion may be subject to controls crafted to protect the individual against arbitrary conduct of governmental authorities, including possible abuses of authority.

4. The interpretation of the phrase "necessary in a democratic society"

When reviewing exercises of State discretion in restricting the operation of rights and freedoms under the Convention, the Court first considers the legality of the act at issue in accordance with the above criteria. Should a State action meet the legality standard, the Convention organs proceed to consider whether the action can also be considered to be "necessary in a democratic society". It is in the review of State compliance with this criterion that the tension between individual and societal interests comes to the fore.

The Court accepts that it has neither the competence nor the need to attempt to exercise practical or political control over State actions within their own domestic spheres. In the case of *Handyside v. the United Kingdom* (1976), it stated:

> By reason of their direct and continuous contact with the vital forces of their countries, State authorities are in principle in a better position than the international judge to give an opinion on the exact content of these requirements ... as well as on the "necessity" of a "restriction" or "penalty" intended to meet them.

It follows from this approach that the Court affords the State a certain degree of discretion to determine the compatibility of a given course of action with the requirements of the Convention. This discretion is commonly referred to as a State's "margin of appreciation".

Although affording the High Contracting Parties to the Convention a margin of appreciation, the Court has reserved to itself the authority to review State exercises of discretion against the principles and limitations set forth not only under the second paragraphs of the relevant Articles, but also under other Articles of the Convention as well (see discussion below on Articles 17 and 18). In the *Handyside* case, the Court stated "The domestic margin of appreciation ... goes hand in hand with a European supervision", a point it has reiterated in a number of cases.

The Court has established that States must attach the "necessary in a democratic society" standard to one of the specific grounds for restrictions listed in the relevant article: a state cannot legitimately invoke general necessity to justify restricting individual rights and freedoms. The grounds for restricting the rights and freedoms listed in the various Articles will be discussed in the following chapters. However, it is important to keep in mind that the Court frames its notion of a democratic society in terms of such concepts as pluralism, tolerance and broadmindedness – none of which is stated in the Convention in so many words (*Handyside*). The Court has also delineated the term "necessary" as being, "not synonymous with 'indispensable', neither has it the flexibility of such expressions as 'admissible', 'ordinary', 'useful', 'reasonable', or 'desirable'" (*Silver, Handyside*).

The Convention organs pursue a two-pronged analysis when determining whether a given State action complies with the "necessary in a democratic society" standard. Firstly, they determine whether the aim of the restriction imposed is itself legitimate. Secondly, they examine whether the means of restricting the right or freedom at issue are "proportionate to the legitimate aim pursued". This requirement is often more difficult for the State to meet. The notion of "necessity" means that any interference with the enjoyment of a protected right must correspond to a pressing social need, and, in particular, must remain proportionate to the legitimate aim pursued. When assessing whether an interference is "necessary", the Court takes into account the margin of appreciation left to the State authorities. However, it considers that it is the duty of the Respondent State to demonstrate the existence of the pressing social need behind a given interference (*McLeod v. the United Kingdom* (1998) and *Klamecki v. Poland (No. 2)* (2003)). When considering whether a state has acted within its margin of appreciation in a given case, the Court may often review the law and practice of other States Parties to the Convention, as well as the facts of the case at issue. Where there appears to be no common ground amongst the states, the Court will afford the respondent state a wide margin of appreciation (*X, Y and Z v. the United Kingdom* (1997)).

In addition to the limitations permitted by the second paragraphs of Articles 8 to 11 and the third paragraph of Article 2 of Protocol No. 4, Articles 17 and 18 may provide independent grounds for restricting or not restricting the enjoyment of the substantive rights set forth in other Articles of the Convention.

5. Prohibition against aiming to destroy or limit Convention rights: Article 17

Article 17

Nothing in this Convention may be interpreted as implying for any State, group or person any right to engage in any activity or perform any act aimed at the destruction of any of the rights and freedoms set forth herein or at their limitation to a greater extent than is provided for in the Convention.

Article 17 of the Convention prohibits States, groups and individuals from acting in any way aimed at the destruction or limitation of the rights and freedoms set forth in the Convention beyond the extent that the Convention itself provides. It follows that Article 17 can only be invoked in connection with an alleged violation of one or more of the substantive rights protected by the Convention.

The structure and operation of Article 17 differ from that of other Articles of the Convention. Article 17 addresses two main types of cases: those in which the State claims that a group or individual has acted in contravention of the principle, and those in which a group or individual claims that the State has infringed its bounds.

When considering the first category of cases under Article 17, it is important to note that when a State invokes the Article against a group or individual, it must claim that the person or group violating the Article thereby affects the rights of a third party. It must also establish that it is invoking Article 17 only in regard to those specific rights which the individual or group are alleged to have abused. Thus in the case of *Lawless v. Ireland* (1961), the Court noted that the United Kingdom could not invoke Article 17 to justify its actions in conjunction with Article 5 (detention) or Article 6 (fair hearing), as the applicant was not abusing or limiting those rights for purposes contrary to the Convention.

In cases in which an individual or group has invoked Article 17 against the State, the Court generally takes the position that if the applicant has also invoked any of the substantive Articles of the Convention that permit limitations on their own terms, the Convention organs will focus their primary examination of the restrictions imposed by the State on those limitations rather than those permitted by Article 17 (see, for example, *Engel and Others v. the Netherlands* (1976)).

In cases raising issues under Articles of the Convention which provide less specific or clear grounds for restricting the exercise of the rights they cover, the Court may review claims of violations of Article 17 more independently. It did so in the case of *Lithgow and Others v. the United Kingdom* (1986), in which the applicants had claimed that the State had violated the right to peaceful enjoyment of property provided under Protocol No. 1, Article 1, and had violated Article 17 in so doing. The Court held that the exercise of State power was compatible with the substantive Article, and that the measures taken were for a legitimate end and were not aimed at the destruction or excessive limitation of the applicants' rights.

In most cases raising claims under Article 17, the Court has taken the position that it is not necessary for it to consider the claim should it have reviewed the same facts in conjunction with another provision of the Convention (see, for example, *Sporrong and Lönnroth v. Sweden* (1982)).

6. Improper application of restrictions clauses: Article 18

Article 18

The restrictions permitted under this Convention to the said rights and freedoms shall not be applied for any purpose other than those for which they have been prescribed.

Article 18 prohibits States from applying permissible restrictions for purposes outside those prescribed by the Convention. Article 18 can only be invoked in connection with one of the substantive rights guaranteed by the Convention. The Court has so far been reluctant to review alleged violations of Article 18 where there has been no violation of the substantive rights invoked (Engel) or where it has examined the operation of the limitations clauses included within the other Articles invoked (*Handyside, Bozano v. France* (1986) and *United Communist Party of Turkey and Others v. Turkey* (1998)).

Chapter 9 – The rights to privacy, family life, home and correspondence, to marry and found a family and to equality of spouses: Article 8, Article 12 and Article 5 of Protocol No. 7

Convention – Article 8

1.   Everyone has the right to respect for his private and family life, his home and his correspondence.

2.   There shall be no interference by a public authority with the exercise of this right except such as is in accordance with the law and is necessary in a democratic society in the interests of national security, public safety or the economic well-being of the country, for the prevention of disorder or crime, for the protection of health or morals, or for the protection of the rights and freedoms of others.

Convention – Article 12

Men and women of marriageable age have the right to marry and to found a family, according to the national laws governing the exercise of this right.

Protocol No. 7 – Article 5

Spouses shall enjoy equality of rights and responsibilities of a private law character between them, and in their relations with their children, as to marriage, during marriage and in the event of its dissolution. This Article shall not prevent States from taking such measures as are necessary in the interests of the children.

The Articles that guarantee respect for privacy, family life, home and correspondence, the right to marry and to found a family and to the equality of spouses protect a wide range of overlapping and interrelated rights. As of the end of 2003, the European Court of Human Rights had not reviewed any claims of violations of Article 5 of Protocol No. 7. However, it had reviewed a number of cases raising claims of violations of rights protected under Article 8 in connection with discrimination, discussed in the chapter entitled "The prohibition against discrimination: Article 14" below.

1. The right to respect

At the outset, it is important to note that the Convention organs have interpreted the right to respect contained in Article 8(1) in light of the stipulation in Article 8(2) that "there shall be no interference by a public authority with the exercise of this right". At first glance, these words appear to mean that the State will be in compliance with its obligations under Article 8 if it simply refrains from acting. The Court has confirmed this primary duty of the State to abstain from interference in the *Belgian Linguistic* case (1968). However, the Convention organs have also extrapolated from the underlying principles of Article 8 a duty for the State to act in order to ensure respect for some rights in some circumstances. The key case in this area is *Marckx v. Belgium* (1979), in which a mother and her natural child challenged Belgian laws which required a mother to take specific action in order to give her child legal status as her daughter, and which continued to exclude such a child from full legal status vis-à-vis other members of the family. The Court found a violation of the right to family life under Article 8, and held:

> When the State determines in its domestic legal system the regime applicable to certain family ties ... it must act in a manner calculated to allow those concerned to lead a normal family life.

The right to respect under Article 8 also comprises the ability for individuals to take legal action with regard to violations of their right to private life (*Airey v. Ireland* (1979) (Irish Government had refused to make available legal aid to a woman wishing to obtain a decree of judicial separation from her violent husband), *X and Y v. the Netherlands* (1985) (disabled adolescent minor lacked the mental capacity to pursue a legal claim against an individual who allegedly had sexually assaulted her, but guardian could not do so either as the minor had reached an age at which she was presumed competent to act on her own behalf)).

2. The nature of private life

The broad interpretation the Court gives to the notion of private life under Article 8 of the Convention includes elements such as gender identification, name, sexual orientation and sexual life. The Article also protects a right to identity and personal development, and the right to establish and develop relationships with other persons and the outside world, including activities of a professional or business nature that may take place in a public context (*Niemietz v. Germany* (1982)).

The right to private life is closely related to the notion of personal integrity. Any interference with the physical integrity of a person must be prescribed by law and requires the consent of that person. Otherwise, a person in a vulnerable situation, such as a detainee, would be deprived of legal guarantees against arbitrary acts. The Court found a violation of the lawfulness requirement of Article 8 in light of these precepts in the case of *Y.F. v. Turkey* (2003), with respect to the compulsory gynaecological examination of the applicant's wife whilst she was in detention.

The right to private life and personal documents

In many States Parties to the Convention, individuals must produce identification documents in the course of essential contacts with governmental authorities or even in daily life. In such circumstances, actions affecting such documents may raise issues with respect to the right to private life under Article 8. Thus, the Court found a violation of this provision in the case of *B v. France* (1992) (in part on the grounds that the State refused to alter the birth register to reflect the change of gender of a transsexual, although French law and practice required the production of a birth certificate when dealing with the authorities on most matters). It also found a violation in the case of *Smirnova v. Russia* (2003), where the State refused to return identity papers to an individual when released from detention on remand, the Court finding that in their everyday life Russian citizens have to prove their identity unusually often, for example when exchanging currency or buying train tickets, as well as in other important contexts, such as applying for jobs or receiving medical care. The Court also noted that not having identity papers is in itself an administrative offence in Russia and that in fact the applicant had been fined for her failure to produce her identity papers.

The rights of homosexuals

The Court has reviewed several cases claiming State violations of the right to privacy through the criminalisation of homosexual activities. In the cases of *Dudgeon v. the United Kingdom* (1981), *Norris v. Ireland* (1988) and *Modinos v. Cyprus* (1993), the Court held that a State's prohibition of homosexual acts between consenting adults constituted an unjustifiable interference with the right to respect for private life under Article 8. The Court also found a violation of Article 8 where an individual had been convicted of a criminal offence with respect to homosexual activities that he had videotaped, but where the likelihood of the videotapes entering the public domain was minimal (*A.D.T. v. the United Kingdom* (2000)). In contrast, the Court found no violation where a government prosecuted certain individuals for engaging in sado-masochistic practices, even if the acts had been consensual (*Laskey, Jaggard and Brown v. the United Kingdom* (1997)). In a line of cases challenging the discharge of several individuals from the British armed services, after their open admissions of their homosexuality and after intrusive investigations into their private lives, the Court also found violations of Article 8 (see, for example, *Lustig-Prean and Beckett v. the United Kingdom* (1999) and *Beck and Others v. the United Kingdom* (2002)).

The rights of transsexuals

In addition to the above-mentioned case of *B. v. France,* the Court has found a violation of the right to private life of transsexuals in the cases of *Christine Goodwin v. the United Kingdom* (2002) (applicant treated as a man with respect to employment-related benefits and unable to marry) and *I. v. the United Kingdom* (2002); and in the case of *Van Kück v. Germany* (2003), the Court found a violation of Article 8 where the State refused to order an insurance company to reimburse the top-up costs of a transsexual's re-assignment treatment. The domestic courts had considered that the applicant was obliged to prove that the treatment was medically necessary, couching their judgments in terms that reflected their belief that the applicant had deliberately caused her transsexual condition.

Environmental conditions and respect for rights guaranteed under Article 8

The Court has reviewed several cases alleging violations of Article 8 due to the failure of governmental authorities adequately to protect private persons against risks to health or life from environmental causes such as the operation of dangerous or polluting activities by the government or businesses. The Court has found violations of Article 8 in cases in which the risks to the health of those in proximity to such activities was clear and where the government failed to take necessary actions to alleviate the effects (*López Ostra v. Spain* (1994) (inactivity of health authorities regarding the nuisance of an unlicensed waste treatment plant near a housing estate, including with respect to related civil and criminal proceedings); *Guerra and Others v. Italy* (1998) (failure of the government to provide the local population with information about risk factors associated with toxic emissions from a nearby chemical factory and how to proceed in the event of accidents)).

Although the Court has reviewed a few cases complaining of violations of Article 8 with respect to the effects of noise pollution from air traffic on private and family life, it has not found any violations (*Powell and Rayner v. the United Kingdom* (1990) and *Hatton and Others v. the United Kingdom* (2003)). Although the Court has established the principle that environmental deterioration stemming from development activities may in some instances affect rights guaranteed under Article 8, in a key case on this issue the Court found that the connection between the activities complained of and the impact on the rights was too tenuous to sustain the claim (*Kyrtatos v. Greece* (2003)).

Bereavement and the right to private and family life

When a State fails to act with sufficient sensitivity to individuals who have suffered the loss of a close relative, the Court may find a violation of Article 8. It did so in the case of *Pannullo and Forte v. France* (2001) where the authorities failed, for a period of seven months, to return the body of a young child who had died in hospital to her parents. The Court found that the French authorities had not struck the right balance between the applicants' right to a private and family life and the need to conduct an effective investigation into the child's death. It also found a violation where the authorities refused to allow an individual who was detained on remand to attend the funerals of his parents (*Ploski v. Poland* (2002)).

3. The nature of family life

As with respect to many other rights guaranteed under the Convention, the European Court of Human Rights gives a broad interpretation of the notion of "family life" under Article 8, finding that its existence is essentially a question of fact depending upon the reality in practice of close personal ties (*K. and T. v. Finland* (2001)). When deciding whether a relationship can be said to amount to "family life", the Court takes into consideration a number of factors such as whether the couple live together, the length of their relationship and whether they have demonstrated their commitment to each other either by having children together or by other means (*Kroon and Others v. the Netherlands* (1994) and *X, Y and Z v. the United Kingdom* (1997)). Children become part of a family unit from the moment of their birth, and the Court considers that the bond established thereby is presumed to be exceptionally strong and thus to require strong reasons for the State to disrupt it (*Berrehab v. the Netherlands* (1988), *Hokkanen v. Finland* (1994), *Gül v. Switzerland* (1996) and *Ciliz v. the Netherlands* (2000)).

The Convention organs have interpreted the term "family life" in Article 8 of the Convention to encompass ties between near relatives, for instance those between grandparents and grandchildren (*Marckx v. Belgium* (1979)). Although the Court has confirmed its view that grandparents may have protected rights under Article 8 of the Convention, for example, in the cases of *Bronda v. Italy* (1998) and *Scozzari and Giunta v. Italy* (2000), it did not find a violation of Article 8 in either case, holding in *Bronda* that the placement of the grandchild for adoption, in light of all the circumstances, fell within the State's margin of appreciation and in *Scozzari and Giunta* that the authorities had acted reasonably in refusing to place grandchildren with their grandmother in Belgium rather than in public care in Italy, where there had been relatively few contacts between them.

Although the Convention organs allow individuals to invoke blood relationships as a starting point for establishing the existence of family life, they do not accept it as the dispositive factor, considering also such factors as the financial or psychological dependency of the parties claiming the right. In general, the Convention organs favour "vertical" family relationships (minor children, parents, grandparents) over "horizontal" ones (siblings, nieces and nephews, etc.). However, in the case of *Olsson v. Sweden* (1988), in which three children had been placed in foster homes at a considerable distance from one another, the Court at least implied that the children could claim a right to family life with each other, independent of their relationship with their parents.

The strongest evidence of the existence of "family life" is proof that those claiming the right already enjoy such a life. However, the Court has held that "this does not mean that all intended family life falls entirely outside [Article 8's] ambit" (*Abdulaziz, Cabales and Balkandali v. the United Kingdom* (1985), in which women who were legally married or engaged had been unable to establish fully normal family life due to discriminatory immigration laws in force in the United Kingdom).

Conversely, the Court has held that the State cannot legitimately act to break up a family unit on the divorce of the parents (*Berrehab v. the Netherlands* (1988) (Moroccan father who had married and divorced in the Netherlands, but had maintained close contacts with his very young daughter and contributed regularly to her material support successfully claimed that a deportation order against him constituted a violation of Article 8)). Similarly, in *Ciliz v. the Netherlands* (2000) the Court found a violation of Article 8 where a Turkish national had permission to reside in the Netherlands with his wife and son, but was given only one year after he and his wife divorced to find a permanent job. On the expiration of the deadline, he was expelled to Turkey although proceedings to determine his access to the child had not been finalised.

Family relationships where parents are not married

Children born out of wedlock

During the life of the Convention, assumptions about the nature of a "family" have changed a great deal, with many children being born to single mothers or unmarried couples, rising divorce rates and similar changes in family structures. As noted above in connection with the *Marckx* case, in such circumstances the Court focuses its analysis under Article 8 primarily on the status and protection of the child within the family unit. For example, in the case of *Johnston and Others v. Ireland* (1986), the Court found that the State was required to ensure that the legal situation of a child born to an Irish couple who were married to others but had lived together for many years was equivalent to that of a child born to a married couple. The Court did not, however, find that Article 8 required Ireland to introduce the possibility of divorce or to otherwise enable the adults to make their own relationship more regular. In a State providing the possibility in law, the Court has, however, found that where a child has established stronger ties with the partner or spouse of a parent than with a biological parent, the Court will consider that the State may legitimately permit that partner or spouse to adopt the child (*Söderbäck v. Sweden* (1998)).

The Court has also held that a child has an independent interest in ascertaining the identity of his or her father. In the case of *Mikulić v. Croatia* (2002), a mother and her daughter, who had been born out of wedlock, filed a paternity suit against the putative father. The man failed both to appear at several court hearings in the case and to abide by court orders to undergo DNA tests for the purpose of determining paternity. In finding a violation of Article 8, the Court found that the State was required to provide alternative means to determine the paternity claim speedily.

Fathers of children born out of wedlock

As with the rights of homosexuals and transsexuals, the Convention case-law relating to the rights of natural fathers has changed considerably over the years. The Court has reviewed several cases raising claims related to the right to family life of natural fathers, finding violations where a child had been surrendered for adoption without the father's knowledge or consent (*Keegan v. Ireland* (1994)) and where a father living as a full member of a family was treated differently from the mother in connection with compulsory care proceedings related to their child (*McMichael v. the United Kingdom* (1995)). Where a father has not maintained regular and sufficient contacts with his young child, however, the State may refuse to allow him to legally recognise him or her (*Yousef v. the Netherlands* (2002)).

The Court has also reviewed several cases involving the rights of natural fathers to have access to their children. In these cases, the Court has placed significant weight on the nature and scope of the fathers' involvement in the decision-making process and on the nature of the government's response to the interests of the fathers (see, for example, *Elsholz v. Germany* (2000), *Sommerfeld v. Germany* (2001), *Sahin v. Germany* (2001) and *Hoffmann v. Germany* (2001)). (See also Chapter 17 below on discrimination.)

Rights when family life has been disrupted

In addition to the changing demographics of the family in Europe, even traditional families may sometimes face disruption, with possible negative implications for the right to family life.

The right to family life of persons in detention

The scope of the right to family life of persons in detention differs according to the reason for the detention; those serving criminal sentences generally have less protection than those detained for other purposes permitted under Article 5 of the Convention. For example, limiting visits to one per month was found to constitute a violation of Article 8 where an individual was detained for the purpose of compelling compliance with a legal obligation and where the individual did not contest the grounds for the detention (*Nowicka v. Poland* (2002)). Even where both spouses have been charged with criminal offences, the Court nevertheless has found that a total prohibition on contact between them for one year was a disproportionate restriction on their rights under Article 8 (*Klamecki v. Poland (No. 2)* (2003)).

Where the executive authorities have total discretion to limit or ban visits or correspondence from family members to prisoners, the Court may find a violation of the requirement under Article 8 that interferences with the right to family life may only be effected "in accordance with law" (*Lavents v. Latvia* (2002), *Poltoratskiy v. Ukraine* (2003) and several other cases against Ukraine). On the other hand, if a legislative body has promulgated guidelines for limiting visits by family members to particular categories of prisoners, the Court may find no violation of Article 8 if the grounds are particularly strong and the possibility of relaxing the restrictions exists (*Messina v. Italy (No. 2)* (2000) (special regime imposed with respect to individuals associated with the Mafia)).

The Court has held that the right to family life under Article 8 does not guarantee the right for convicted prisoners to enjoy conjugal visits with their spouses (*Aliev v. Ukraine* (2003)).

Custody and access

Difficult relationships between separated or divorced parents may often lead the custodial spouse to create obstacles to access to children by the non-custodial parent. Although the Court will generally defer to a State's determination as to which parent or other relative should have custody of a child on the divorce of the parents, should a State fail to implement any right to access by the parent without custody, there may be a violation of Article 8 (*Hokkanen v. Finland* (1994) and *Hansen v. Turkey* (2003)). However, as long as the State makes good faith efforts to enforce access arrangements, the Court will not find a violation of Article 8 where the primary obstacle to access is the conduct of the custodian of the child (*Glaser v. the United Kingdom* (2000) and *Nuutinen v. Finland* (2000)). In the same vein, where one parent abducts a child, making it impossible for the other parent and the child to exercise their right to family life, the Court will find a violation of Article 8 if it finds that the competent authorities have failed to locate the child, to restore the rights that were restricted and to penalise the parent who has wrongfully removed and retained the child (*Ignacollo-Zenide v. Romania* (2000) and *Maire v. Portugal* (2003)); and should both States involved in an international parental abduction be parties to the Hague Convention of 25 October 1980 on the Civil Aspects of International Child Abduction, which dictates actions to be taken in such cases, the Court may take this into consideration in its review of the case before it, as it did when it found a violation of Article 8 in the cases of *Iglesias Gil and A.U.I. v. Spain* (2003) and *Sylvester v. Austria* (2003).

Children in public care

The Court has consistently held that the taking of children into public care, however legitimate the taking may be, should normally be regarded as a temporary measure, with the ultimate aim of actions taken during the period that a child has been taken into public care being the reunification of the family and the discontinuance of public care as soon as feasible (*Eriksson v. Sweden* (1989), *Johansen v. Norway* (1996) and *K.A. v. Finland* (2003)). The State has a positive duty to implement these principles, subject always to its being balanced against its duty to consider the best interests of the child (*K. and T. v. Finland* (2001)). Although the co-operation of the parents with the responsible authorities is a factor that may be taken into account when determining whether or not there has been a violation of Article 8, it is not the sole factor, as the authorities nevertheless have a duty to implement measures that will be apt to enable family links to be maintained (*Olsson v. Sweden* (1988), *E.P. v. Italy* (1999) and *Gnahoré v. France* (2000)). Not only must the authorities place a time-limit on any care order affecting the right to family life, they must also ensure that the manner in which they handle contacts between parents and children during that period serves to foster positive relationships between them (*Scozzari and Giunta v. Italy* (2000)).

In some cases, the Court has found that even the taking of children into public care has contravened the right to family life protected under Article 8. For example, in the case of *Kutzner v. Germany* (2002), the State had removed children from their parents in part on the grounds of their late development, although the parents, who were of limited intellectual capacities, had requested and received some educational support for the children. During the course of the family's relationship with the authorities, all experts had certified that the parents had neither neglected nor abused their children and several had recommended the reunification of the family. The Court found a violation of Article 8 with respect to both the placement order and its implementation.

Although the Court may defer to the State with respect to the wisdom of taking children into care, it may nevertheless find a violation of Article 8 where the State had provided the parents with an inadequate opportunity to participate in the proceedings through which the decisions had been taken to place or keep the child outside the family environment, and, in some instances, to deny the parents the right of access (*O., H., W., B., and R.* (all *v. the United Kingdom*) (1987), *Olsson v. Sweden* (1988), *Buchberger v. Austria* (2001), *T.P. and K.M. v. the United Kingdom* (2001) and *Venema v. the Netherlands* (2002)). In proceedings concerning children, time takes on a particular significance as there is a danger that any procedural delay may result in the de facto determination of the disposition of the relevant issues (*H. v. the United Kingdom* (1987) and *Covezzi and Morselli v. Italy* (2003)). Note that many of the cases raising claims of violations of the right to family life in connection with the taking of children into public care also raise claims of violations of the right to fair proceedings under Article 6 (see also Chapter 6 above).

Although the European Court of Human Rights has accepted that in some instances children may need to be removed from the care of their parents, in two cases it has found the removal of a newborn from its mother to be too extreme a measure to be compatible with Article 8 of the Convention, even should the mother have a history of mental disturbances, difficult family relationships or similar personal problems (see, for example, *K. and T. v Finland* (2001)). In the case of *P., C. and S. v. the United Kingdom* (2002), the Court also found a violation of Article 8 with respect to the speed with which the competent authorities acted to free a newborn baby for adoption after its removal from its mother, coupled with the failure of the authorities to provide adequate opportunity for the parents to participate fully in the decision-making process.

Family life: immigration and expulsion

Article 1 of the European Convention on Human Rights requires States Parties to secure Convention rights and freedoms to everyone within their jurisdiction, not just to citizens. The realisation of this principle is perhaps most clear in the line of cases raising claims of violation of the right to family life where a State acts to deport or revoke the residence permit of an individual from a non-State Party who has established family life with a national of a State Party. In determining whether such an action may constitute a violation of the right to family life, the European Court of Human Rights considers a number of factors. Note that as each case the Court has reviewed under this head comprises a complex set of factors, it is difficult to derive any clear guiding principles from the case-law.

The majority of cases challenging a deportation order have been brought by men who have been convicted of one or more criminal offences in a State Party and who face deportation at the conclusion of their prison sentences. In such cases, the Court will take into consideration not only the number or seriousness of the crimes committed but also the personal circumstances of the individual. Where he has no real connection with the country to which he is to be sent and/or very strong connections to family residing in the country wishing to deport him, the Court will find a violation (*Moustaquim v. Belgium* (1991), *Beldjoudi v. France* (1992), *Nasri v. France* (1995), *Amrollahi v. Denmark* (2002) and *Jakupovic v. Austria* (2003) (deportation of a 16-year-old to Bosnia and Herzegovina, where he had no close relatives)). Where connections with the country to which an applicant may be removed do exist, however, the Court will normally defer to the State's judgment in the matter (*C. v. Belgium* (1996), *Boughanemi v. France* (1996) and *Boujlifa v. France* (1997)).

In cases in which no criminal offence has been committed, the Court is inclined to find no violation of Article 8 in circumstances in which the family whose life together may be disrupted by the removal of one parent from the country may reasonably be expected to establish and maintain a family life in that parent's home country (*Gül v. Switzerland* (1996) (refusal by Swiss authorities to permit minor son of a Turkish citizen who held a residence permit issued on humanitarian grounds to join him in Switzerland on the grounds that the entire family could go back to Turkey)). However, where the spouse of a non-national may face severe difficulties in the other country, the Court has taken the view that separating the couple constitutes a violation of Article 8 (*Boultif v. Switzerland* (2001) (Swiss woman could not be expected to follow her husband to Algeria, given her lack of language skills and other factors)).

The Court has found that where the intention to maintain family ties and life exists, the State must present strong reasons for either disrupting relations between a parent and a child or preventing family reunification (*Berrehab v. the Netherlands* (1988) ("economic well-being of the country" an insufficient justification to refuse to permit the Moroccan father of a child with whom he had an ongoing relationship to remain in the country) and *Sen v. the Netherlands* (2001) (violation of Article 8 for refusal to issue a residence permit to a child living with relatives in Turkey but whose parents and two other siblings were long-term residents of the Netherlands)).

Even when a convicted criminal has very strong ties with the deporting country, the Court may find no violation of Article 8 (*Bouchelkia v. France* (1997) (individual deported following a criminal conviction for rape had come to France at the age of two, had a large family lawfully resident there, and had declared paternity of a child by a French woman whom he married) and *Dalia v. France* (1998) (order permanently excluding from French territory a convicted Algerian woman who had arrived in France as a teenager to join her large family and who was the mother of a minor child of French nationality)). On the other hand, it has found violations of Article 8 on similar facts (*Yilmaz v. Germany* (2003) (foreign national born in Germany, living there his entire life and the father of a young child with a German national deported for having committed several serious offences while a juvenile and indefinitely excluded from the territory) and *Yildiz v. Austria* (2002) (expulsion of foreigner following convictions, resulting in separation from wife and child)).

Immigration and deportation issues related to the changing configuration of European states have only recently been raised before the European Court of Human Rights. In the case of *Slivenko v. Latvia* (2003), a woman of Russian origin who had lived almost her entire life in Latvia married a Russian army officer with whom she had a child. On Latvia's independence, the family were registered as "ex-USSR citizens". Subsequently, the husband was required to leave Latvia as part of a treaty agreement on the withdrawal of Russian troops. The authorities thus annulled the registration of the applicants and ordered their deportation. They were then evicted from their flat, arrested and briefly detained in a centre for illegal immigrants. Although they ultimately left Latvia and adopted Russian citizenship, the terms of their deportation order meant that they could not return to Latvia for five years and then for only up to ninety days at a time, effectively prohibiting them from visiting the first applicant's parents. The Court found a violation of Article 8.

As discussed in a previous chapter, where an individual who is subject to deportation alleges he or she will be ill-treated in the country of return, the Court will demand that the State assess that possibility independently from all other factors.

4. Privacy, correspondence and the home: surveillance and data collection

The Convention organs have reviewed a number of cases claiming that the State's surveillance of private individuals or its collection and use of personal data violates one or more of the provisions of Article 8(1) of the Convention – the right to respect for privacy, correspondence and/or the home. In the case of *Klass and Others v. Germany* (1978) the applicants complained that a statutory regime that permitted the authorities to conduct surveillance activities against individuals without informing them that such surveillance had been conducted constituted a violation of the right to privacy under Article 8. The Court held that the domestic statute governing surveillance was sufficiently precise, and that the procedures for ensuring that any measure of surveillance would comply with its conditions were strict enough to comply with the legality requirements of Article 8(2). The Court also held that the State's need to protect against "imminent dangers" threatening "the free democratic constitutional order" were legitimate State aims under the "necessary in a democratic society in the interests of national security [and] for the prevention of disorder or crime" provision. Finally, the Court found that the aforementioned procedures were adequate to guarantee that any State actions would be proportionate to those legitimate aims. In *Malone v. the United Kingdom* (1984), the applicants complained that secret surveillance against them, in the course of criminal investigations, violated their rights to privacy and correspondence (in this context defined to encompass all forms of private communications) under Article 8. At issue in the case were police interception of phone calls (wiretapping) and the maintenance of a "register" of numbers dialled from a particular telephone (metering). The Court found that the United Kingdom statute regulating wiretapping was too vague to be "in accordance with law" in the sense of Article 8. The Court further held that although metering itself was a legitimate and normal business practice, unlike wiretapping, the provision of metering records to the police, without legal regulation or the consent of the person being metered, constituted an unjustifiable interference with the right to privacy under Article 8.

As with respect to other Articles of the Convention (see, for example, the discussion above in Chapter 5 on the right to liberty), in the event that the Court finds that the State has not applied its own domestic law with respect to surveillance or other information gathering activities, it will find a violation of Article 8 (*Perry v. the United Kingdom* (2003)).

Following on from the key cases of *Klass* and *Malone*, the Court has found a number of violations of Article 8 on the grounds that the legal and/or regulatory regimes governing the tapping of telephones have not met the standards of lawfulness required under the Convention (see, for example, *Huvig v. France* (1990), *Kruslin v. France* (1990), *Valenzuela Contreras v. Spain* (1998), *Khan v. the United Kingdom* (2000), *Prado Bugallo v. Spain* (2003), *M.M. v. the Netherlands* (2003), *Armstrong v. the United Kingdom* (2002) and *Hewitson v. the United Kingdom* (2003)). The location of the telephone has no bearing on the applicability of Article 8 (*Kopp v. Switzerland* (1998) and *Amann v. Switzerland* (2000) (applies to business premises such as law offices), *Lambert v. France* (1998) (applies to telephone calls made on lines belonging to third parties) and *Halford v. the United Kingdom* (1997) (applies to employees of the police department making telephone calls from police headquarters)). The Court has also held that the principles governing wiretapping also apply to intercepting messages on other types of communications technology, for example, personal pagers (*Taylor-Sabori v. the United Kingdom* (2002)).

Surveillance and monitoring of persons in public places does not automatically lead to the finding of a violation of Article 8, although the protections of the Article will be triggered in the event that inadequate controls are exercised over the retention and use of material obtained through these processes. With respect to the retention of private information obtained by the authorities, the Court has found a violation of Article 8 where governmental security services have compiled data on particular individuals even without the unlawful use of covert surveillance methods (*Rotaru v. Romania* (2000) and *Amann v. Switzerland* (2000)). With respect to the use of private information obtained by the authorities, the Court has found a violation of Article 8 where information that had been legitimately obtained had been released into the public domain without adequate oversight to ensure that the privacy of the individual was respected (*Craxi v. Italy* (*No. 2*) (2003) (authorities failed both to control access by the press to transcripts of private telephone calls and to fulfil legal requirements for the determination of material from the telephone calls that could be publicly read out at trial) and *Peck v. the United Kingdom* (2003) (disclosure to the public of closed circuit television images in which a mentally disturbed individual could be identified)).

Specific issues under Article 8 arise in connection with criminal investigations, as alluded to above. The Court has found violations of this provision where the police used covert devices to record the voices of persons answering police questions, saved the recordings for further analysis and used the analysis at trial, all without informing the individuals of the actions taken during the investigations process (*P.G. and J.H. v. the United Kingdom* (2001), where the police had coached and planted an informant in an individual's cell and used covert audio and video surveillance in the cell, the prison visiting area and on a fellow prisoner and where the authorities had used the information gained through these methods at his trial (*Allan v. United Kingdom* (2002)). The Court has also found violations of Article 8 where a private citizen made a clandestine recording of a telephone conversation with the help of a high-ranking police officer (*A. v. France* (1993)).

The cases of *Gaskin v. the United Kingdom* (1989) and *M.G. v. the United Kingdom* (2002) concerned the State's failure to respond effectively to the applicants' requests for access to their social service case records and to ensure that any refusal of such access could be challenged before an independent body. The Court found a violation of Article 8 in both cases. In contrast, the Court considered that a balance must be struck between the rights of parents surrendering infants for adoption and the rights of the child to obtain information about them. Noting that the States have a wide margin of appreciation in this area, the Court found no violation of Article 8 where authorities refused to release such information in a case in which the natural mother had both requested secrecy and surrendered all parental rights (*Odièvre v. France* (2003)).

Finally, in the case of *Z v. Finland* (1997), the Court held that placing a time limit on the confidentiality of an individual's medical records could lead to a violation of Article 8 should the records be made public at the end of the relevant period. It further held that the publication of the individual's name and medical condition in a public judgment, where domestic law allowed for the possibility of keeping information confidential, also constituted a violation of Article 8.

5. The right to respect for the home

The Convention organs have reviewed cases claiming violations of the right to respect for the home with respect to several types of issue. The Court has held that an individual can be considered to have established a home in the sense of Article 8 even if he or she has done so in contravention of domestic law (*Buckley v. the United Kingdom* (1996)). An individual may also claim a right to respect for the home in regard to a property he or she occupies for significant periods each year (*Menteş and Others v. Turkey* (1997)). Offices and other business premises fall within the purview of this head under Article 8 (*Niemietz v. Germany* (1992), *Roemen and Schmit v. Luxembourg* (2003) and *Stes Colas Est and Others v. France* (2002)) as may automobiles in some instances (*Ernst and Others v. Belgium* (2003)).

In the above-mentioned *Menteş* case and a number of similar cases, the Court has found violations of the right to respect for the home where the homes of the applicants had allegedly been burned down or otherwise destroyed by Turkish security forces and where the government offered no alternative explanation for their destruction (see, for example, *Selçuk and Asker v. Turkey* (1998) and *Bilgin v. Turkey* (2000)).

The Court has reviewed several cases regarding the right to remain in one's home or to gain access to one's home. In a series of cases brought against the United Kingdom, starting with the above-mentioned *Buckley* case, Roma applicants have alleged violations of Article 8 in the government's refusal to allow them to station their caravans on land for which they did not have permission to establish residences or place buildings. The Court has consistently found that the "affirmative obligation" under Article 8 of States towards the Roma does not extend to the implementation of a general social policy for the accommodation of their distinctive housing needs. Nor does the State have an obligation to provide suitable housing for Roma families unable to maintain homes in their chosen location. (See also *Chapman* (2001), *Beard* (2001), *Coster* (2001), *Lee* (2001) and *Jane Smith* (2001) all *v. the United Kingdom.*)

The Court found a continuing violation of Article 8 in the inter-State case of *Cyprus v. Turkey* (2001) in the refusal of the Turkish Government to allow the return of any Greek Cypriot displaced persons to their homes in northern Cyprus (in addition to a violation of Article 8, "from an overall standpoint", of the rights of Greek Cypriots living in northern Cyprus to respect for their private and family life and to respect for their home). In the case of *Gillow v. the United Kingdom* (1986), the Court held that the State's refusal to grant the applicants a licence to occupy their own house violated Article 8 in that it was disproportionate to the otherwise legitimate aim of ensuring the economic well-being of the Island of Guernsey.

Although the conduct of criminal investigations and the implementation of certain civil court decisions may provide grounds for the authorities to enter someone's private home, the Court has consistently held that such entries must be both lawful and proportionate under Article 8. It has found violations of Article 8 on the grounds that the requirements of lawfulness were not met in the cases of *Funke v. France* (1993), *Crémieux v. France* (1993) and *Miailhe v. France* (1993), regarding house searches made by customs officers who had broad discretion to conduct such searches and who were not subject to judicial supervision.

In the case of *Chappell v. the United Kingdom* (1989), the Court found no violation of Article 8 where the United Kingdom authorities had permitted the simultaneous execution of a police search warrant and a court order allowing the plaintiffs in a civil suit against the applicant to search his home and offices. Neither did it find a violation where properly authorised police entered an individual's home for the purpose of effecting an arrest (*Murray v. the United Kingdom* (1994)).

The Court found a violation of Article 8 where the homes of individuals were searched under a warrant framed in very wide terms, with no additional information being provided to them about the reasons for the searches, and where no criminal investigation against them had been undertaken (*Ernst and Others v. Belgium* (2003)). Where the police assist a third party in entering a private home, the Court has found that they are under an obligation to ensure that all parties have agreed to such entry, or that a valid court order exists authorising the action (*McLeod v. the United Kingdom* (1998) (police assisted ex-husband of applicant and his solicitor to enter the former matrimonial home and remove property therefrom prior to a court-ordered deadline for the delivery of the property in connection with divorce proceedings)).

6. The right to respect for correspondence

The majority of cases claiming violations of the right to respect for correspondence have been raised by prisoners. The Court has held that a prisoner's right to uncensored correspondence with a lawyer or judicial body is almost inviolate as the principal means by which the individual may seek the vindication of his rights (*Golder v. the United Kingdom* (1975), *Campbell v. the United Kingdom* (1992), *Domenichini v. Italy* (1996) and *Calogero Diana v. Italy* (1996)). The Court takes a particularly strong position on this issue where the authorities censor, monitor or obstruct correspondence between a detainee and Convention institutions (see, for example, *Salapa v. Poland* (2002), *Messina v. Italy (No. 2)* (2000) and No. 3 (2002), *Valašinas v. Lithuania* (2001), *A.B. v. the Netherlands* (2002), *Klamecki v. Poland (No. 2)* (2003) and *Matwiejczuk v. Poland* (2003)).

De facto obstruction of a detainee's correspondence with judicial or other governmental authorities may also lead to the finding of a violation of Article 8 of the Convention. It did so in the case of *William Faulkner v. the United Kingdom* (2002), in which the Court found that no legitimate grounds existed for the failure of prison authorities to post a letter from the applicant to the Scottish Minister of State and in the case of *Cotlet v. Romania* (2003), in which prison authorities had refused to provide a prisoner with writing materials, delayed in transmitting his correspondence to Convention institutions and controlled all such correspondence.

The Court has generally permitted States to impose at least some restrictions on correspondence to and from detainees that is not of a legal nature. In the case of *Silver and Others v. United Kingdom* (1983), the Court held that the State could reasonably censor letters referring to the presence in a given prison of certain dangerous prisoners, the conduct of illegal business practices, and other similar topics. However, general control of the correspondence of someone accused of particularly serious offences, where such control is for an unlimited time and for no more specific reasons, will contravene Article 8 (*Lavents v. Latvia* (2002)). Similarly, the exercise of too broad a discretion to control general correspondence, coupled with the lack of any independent review process, will be unacceptable (*Petra v. Romania* (1998) (prison authorities had the power not to deliver to a prisoner any letter or any newspaper, book or magazine "unsuited to the process of rehabilitating a prisoner", such decisions not being amenable to appeal)).

In a unique case, the Court found a violation of Article 8 where prison authorities in the Dutch Antilles prohibited all correspondence between prisoners who had been released and those still in detention (*A.B. v. the Netherlands* (2002)).

Although the majority of European Court of Human Rights cases raising claims of violation of the right to respect for correspondence have come from detainees, the Court has occasionally reviewed cases on this issue arising in other contexts. The Court found a violation of this provision of Article 8 where the Swedish Government restricted communications by telephone or correspondence between a mother and her son who had been taken into public care (*Margareta and Roger Andersson v. Sweden* (1992)). It also has found violations in several cases where restrictions have been placed on the correspondence of individuals or businesses going through bankruptcy proceedings. For example, the Court found a violation where a trustee in bankruptcy had opened letters between the bankrupt applicant and his legal advisers, in part during a period of time during which the trustee did not have any valid legal authority to do so (*Foxley v. the United Kingdom* (2000)) and where restrictions were placed on the receipt of correspondence by bankrupts for long periods of time (*Luordo v. Italy* (2003) and *Bassani v. Italy* (2003)).

7. The right to marry and found a family: Article 12

The Court has reviewed relatively few cases complaining of violations of the right to marry and found a family. As noted above, Article 12 does not guarantee the right to divorce and/or remarry (*Johnston and Others v. Ireland* (1986)). Although for a number of years the Court was unwilling to find a violation of Article 12 where a State has refused to facilitate the marriage of transsexuals to a person of the newly-opposite sex (see, for example, *Rees v. the United Kingdom* (1986), *Cossey v. the United Kingdom* (1990) and *Sheffield and Horsham v. the United Kingdom* (1998)), it finally did so in the cases of *Christine Goodwin v. the United Kingdom* (2002) and *I. v. the United Kingdom* (2002), referring to major social changes in the institution of marriage since the adoption of the Convention as well as dramatic changes brought about by developments in medicine and science in the field of transsexuality.

In the case of *F. v. Switzerland* (1987), the Court held that the temporary prohibition on remarriage of a man who had been married and divorced three times within eighteen years, but who wished to contract a fourth marriage, constituted a violation of the right to marry under Article 12. However, it found no violation of this provision where an individual claimed that the length of divorce proceedings – more than seventeen years – had unduly delayed the possibility of starting a new family, where no facts were adduced supporting either the existence of or plan for a new family (*Berlin v. Luxembourg* (2003)).

Chapter 10 – Freedom of thought, conscience and religion: Article 9

Article 9

> 1.   Everyone has the right to freedom of thought, conscience and religion; this right includes freedom to change his religion or belief and freedom, either alone or in community with others and in public or in private, to manifest his religion or belief, in worship, teaching, practice and observance.
>
> 2.   Freedom to manifest one's religion or beliefs shall be subject only to such limitations as are prescribed by law and are necessary in a democratic society in the interests of public safety, for the protection of public order, health or morals, or for the protection of the rights and freedoms of others.

The terms "thought", "belief", "conscience" and "religion" may cover a wide range of intellectual and spiritual activity. The rights to freedom of thought, conscience and religion are largely exercised inside an individual's heart and mind. It is only when one manifests one's thoughts or beliefs that the state will become aware of their existence or character. But at that very point, a given manifestation may also raise issues in the realm of freedom of expression (Article 10) or another Article of the Convention. Where a case raises issues under Article 9 in addition to other Articles, review will often be limited to alleged violations of those other Articles.

The Court described the importance of the rights guaranteed under Article 9 of the Convention in the case of *Kokkinakis v. Greece* (1993):

> [A]s enshrined in Article 9, freedom of thought, conscience and religion is one of the foundations of a "democratic society" within the meaning of the Convention. It is, in its religious dimension, one of the most vital elements that go to make up the identity of believers and their conception of life, but it is also a precious asset for atheists, agnostics, sceptics and the unconcerned. The pluralism indissociable from a democratic society, which has been dearly won over the centuries, depends on it. (paragraph 31)

In clarifying the terms listed in Article 9, the Court has rejected the argument that because "thought" and language are so closely intertwined, any State restrictions on the use of one's chosen language constitutes an interference with freedom of thought under Article 9 (*Belgian Linguistic* case (1968)). No distinctions are normally drawn between the terms "conscience" and "belief", but the Convention institutions have generally accepted an individual applicant's assertion that a given idea or intellectual position falls within their purview. However, the manifestation of a belief may fall outside the protection of Article 9(1) where the act at issue is not a manifestation of the belief itself, but has only been motivated or influenced by it (*Kalaç v. Turkey* (1997)).

1. Interference by the State in the internal affairs of religious institutions

In recent years, the Court has found violations of Article 9 where States have intervened in the organisation or internal affairs of religious groups. In the cases of *Serif v. Greece* (1999) and *Agga v. Greece (No. 2)* (2002), for example, the applicants had been convicted of the criminal offence of "usurping the functions of a minister of a known religion and publicly wearing the dress of such a minister". The applicants in these cases had been elected as a mufti within their communities. The government, however, had appointed other individuals to the same functions. In finding the violations of Article 9, the Court found that where a group of individuals voluntarily follows someone as a religious leader, it is incompatible with the demands of religious pluralism in a democratic society to punish that leader. The Court also stressed that it could not be considered necessary in a democratic society for the State to take measures to ensure that religious communities have a unified leadership. In responding to concern expressed by the State that divisions within communities may lead to tension, the Court made the following observation:

> Although the Court recognises that it is possible that tension is created in situations where a religious or any other community becomes divided, it considers that this is one of the unavoidable consequences of pluralism. The role of the authorities in such circumstances is not to remove the cause of tension by eliminating pluralism, but to ensure that the competing groups tolerate each other (...) (*Agga v. Greece (No. 2)* (2002)) (paragraph 60)

Similar facts arose in the case of *Hasan and Chaush v. Bulgaria* (2000), in which the Court found a violation of Article 9 where the government had intervened in the organisation and leadership of the Muslim communities in Bulgaria, for example, by refusing to register certain decisions taken at a national conference of Muslims, such as the election of the Chief Mufti and changes to the internal statute of the group, and by registering a rival group as the sole representative organisation of the faith in Bulgaria and permitting that rival group to forcibly evict the applicants from their offices on the strength of that registration. The Court stated:

> [R]eligious communities traditionally and universally exist in the form of organised structures. They abide by rules which are often seen by followers as being of a divine origin. Religious ceremonies have their meaning and sacred value for the believers if they have been conducted by ministers empowered for that purpose in compliance with these rules. The personality of the religious ministers is undoubtedly of importance to every member of the community. Participation in the life of the community is thus a manifestation of one's religion, protected by Article 9 of the Convention.

> Where the organisation of the religious community is at issue, Article 9 of the Convention must be interpreted in the light of Article 11, which safeguards associative life against unjustified State interference. Seen in this perspective, the believers' right to freedom of religion encompasses the expectation that the community will be allowed to function peacefully, free from arbitrary State

intervention. Indeed, the autonomous existence of religious communities is indispensable for pluralism in a democratic society and is thus an issue at the very heart of the protection which Article 9 affords. It directly concerns not only the organisation of the community as such but also the effective enjoyment of the right to freedom of religion by all its active members. Were the organisational life of the community not protected by Article 9 of the Convention, all other aspects of the individual's freedom of religion would become vulnerable. (paragraph 57)

2. Interference with the establishment or operation of religious institutions

The Court has held that a church or ecclesiastical body may, as such, exercise on behalf of its adherents the rights guaranteed by Article 9 of the Convention (*Cha'are Shalom Ve Tsedek v. France* (2000) and *Metropolitan Church of Bessarabia and Others v. Moldova* (2001)). It has found violations of Article 9 with respect to religious bodies as such where a State has denied legal status to particular churches or religious associations. For example, in the case of *Metropolitan Church of Bessarabia and Others v. Moldova* (2001), the government refused to grant legal recognition to the applicant church, on the grounds that its members could freely practise their religion within the legally recognised Metropolitan Church of Moldova. The government thereby prevented the applicant church from operating, its priests from conducting divine service and its members from meeting to practise their religion. By denying it a legal personality, the government also prevented the Church from being able to enjoy judicial protection of its assets. The Court stated:

> [I]n principle the right to freedom of religion for the purposes of the Convention excludes assessment by the State of the legitimacy of religious beliefs or the ways in which those beliefs are expressed. State measures favouring a particular leader or specific organs of a divided religious community or seeking to compel the community or part of it to place itself, against its will, under a single leadership, would also constitute an infringement of the freedom of religion. In democratic societies the State does not need to take measures to ensure that religious communities remain or are brought under a unified leadership.... Similarly, where the exercise of the right to freedom of religion or of one of its aspects is subject under domestic law to a system of prior authorisation, involvement in the procedure for granting authorisation of a recognised ecclesiastical authority cannot be reconciled with the requirements of paragraph 2 of Article 9. (citations deleted) (paragraph 117)

The Court has found a number of violations of Article 9 where States have promulgated laws, issued decrees or instituted practices which have afforded the State powers to obstruct the free manifestation of religious belief. In the case of *Manoussakis and Others v. Greece* (1996), the applicants had been convicted for establishing and operating a place of worship without proper governmental authorisation. The Court noted that in spite of the applicants' concerted attempts to obtain the necessary authorisation, the responsible authorities had indefinitely deferred taking a decision on the matter. It there-fore found that basing a criminal conviction on a failure to comply with legal formalities, where the State was remiss in fulfilling its own role in this regard, constituted a violation of Article 9.

In the inter-State case of *Cyprus v. Turkey* (2001), the Court found a violation of Article 9 in that restrictions placed on the freedom of movement of some Greek Cypriots remaining in the northern part of Cyprus had curtailed their ability to observe their religious beliefs by restricting their access to places of worship outside their villages and their participation in other aspects of religious life.

The applicant association in the case of *Cha'are Shalom Ve Tsedek v. France* (2000) complained that the refusal of the competent authorities to grant their religious association permission to engage in a particular method of ritual slaughter of animals for food consumption constituted a violation of their right to freedom of religion. The Court considered that because the applicant association could obtain meat slaughtered in accordance with the required ritual from other sources that there had been no interference with rights protected under Article 9.

3. The rights of individuals to manifest their beliefs

In the case of *Kokkinakis v. Greece* (1993), the Court found a violation of Article 9 where the government could not show that the applicant, who had been convicted of proselytism, had used improper methods in discussing his religious beliefs with others. In the later case of *Larissis and Others v. Greece* (1998), the Court again found a violation of Article 9 where officers in the Greek military had been prosecuted for engaging in the proselytising of civi-lians, finding that no improper pressure had been applied in the circum-stances. However, it found no violation of the Article with respect to their convictions for the proselytising of soldiers under their command, finding that the State could legitimately introduce special measures to protect the rights of subordinates, given the risk of their harassment within the hierar-chical structure of the military. In the same vein, the Court found no viola-tion of Article 9 where the State compelled a military judge to retire from his post on the grounds that some aspects of his conduct had breached military discipline and had infringed the principle of secularism upon which the mili-tary was based. The Court noted that there had been no interference by the State in the exercise of the applicant's religious beliefs, as the conduct upon which the compulsory retirement decision was based could not be consi-dered a manifestation of those beliefs (*Kalaç v. Turkey* (1997)).

The Court has held that a State may not compel individuals to manifest reli-gious beliefs as a precondition of holding electoral office (*Buscarini and Others v. San Marino* (1999) (elected governmental representatives were required to swear an oath on the Gospels or to forfeit their parliamentary seats)).

Where the laws and regulations governing detention regimes do not provide clear guidance about the rights of detainees to attend religious services, receive visits from priests or otherwise to manifest their religious beliefs, the Court has found a violation of Article 9 on the grounds that such lack of clarity is not "in accordance with law" (*Poltoratskiy v. Ukraine* (2003) and *Kuznetsov v. Ukraine* (2003)).

Chapter 11 – Freedom of expression and information: Article 10

Article 10

1.   Everyone has the right to freedom of expression. This right shall include freedom to hold opinions and to receive and impart information and ideas without interference by public authority and regardless of frontiers. This Article shall not prevent States from requiring the licensing of broadcasting, television or cinema enterprises.

2.   The exercise of these freedoms, since it carries with it duties and responsibilities, may be subject to such formalities, conditions, restrictions or penalties as are prescribed by law and are necessary in a democratic society, in the interests of national security, territorial integrity or public safety, for the prevention of disorder or crime, for the protection of health or morals, for the protection of the reputation or rights of others, for preventing the disclosure of information received in confidence, or for maintaining the authority and impartiality of the judiciary.

The right to freedom of expression is not only a primary cornerstone of democracy, but also a prerequisite for the enjoyment of many of the other rights and freedoms enshrined in the Convention. Because of its importance, many of the cases that have established standards of interpretation for the underlying principles of the Convention have arisen under Article 10.

1. The scope of the term "expression" under Article 10

Article 10 states that the right to freedom of expression "shall include freedom to hold opinions and to receive and impart information and ideas". In the case of *Handyside v. the United Kingdom* (1976), the Court considered whether the conviction of an individual who had published a reference book for schoolchildren that contained advice on sexual and other matters, constituted a violation of his rights under Article 10. Although the Court held that the State was acting within its margin of appreciation in invoking the "protection of morals" clause under the second paragraph, the Court nevertheless stated its position on the role of the right to freedom of expression in a democratic society:

> Freedom of expression constitutes one of the essential foundations of such a society, one of the basic conditions for its progress and for the development of every man.... It is applicable not only to "information" or "ideas" that are favourably received or regarded as inoffensive or as a matter of indifference, but also to those that offend, shock or disturb the State or any sector of the population. Such are the demands of that pluralism, tolerance and broadmindedness without which there is no "democratic society".

101

2. The hierarchy of values served by Article 10

Although it may sometimes be unclear, the European Court of Human Rights has established a rough hierarchy of values to be served by Article 10, protecting different categories of expression to differing degrees. Within this hierarchy, commentary on public matters by public figures or the media constitute the most protected forms of expression; commercial expression the least.

3. Freedom of expression in the context of public debate

The Court places a high value on the exercise of freedom of expression by elected members of legislatures, holding that they must be provided broad protection to express themselves on matters of interest to their constituencies and to the public in general. In this regard, the Court found a violation of Article 10 in a case in which a member of parliament had been convicted of insulting the government (*Castells v. Spain* (1992)). It did so again in a case in which an elected representative had been subject to an injunction against expressing negative views about private associations that were active in a public debate on a controversial political issue (*Jerusalem v. Austria* (2001)). Drawing an analogy with individuals who actively engage in public debate, the Court considered that associations that choose to do so should have a high degree of tolerance to criticism from their opponents.

Public and political figures themselves, however, must be open to criticism from the media. The Court has heard a number of cases in which senior members of government or elected representatives have won defamation cases in the domestic courts, regularly finding such actions in violation of Article 10 of the Convention. In the leading cases of *Lingens v. Austria* (1986), *Oberschlick v. Austria* (*No. 1*) (1991) and *Oberschlick v. Austria* (*No. 2*) (1997), editors of political periodicals had published articles criticising politicians for their public statements on policy issues. Each of the politicians brought private defamation actions against the applicants, all of which were successful. The applicants claimed that the decisions of the Austrian courts infringed their freedom of expression under Article 10. The Court agreed, noting in the *Lingens* case that:

> Freedom of the press ... affords the public one of the best means of discovering and forming an opinion of the ideas and attitudes of political leaders. More generally, freedom of political debate is at the very core of the concept of a democratic society which prevails throughout the Convention.

> The limits of acceptable criticism are accordingly wider as regards a politician as such than as regards a private individual. Unlike the latter, the former inevitably and knowingly lays himself open to close scrutiny of his every word and deed by both journalists and the public at large.... Article 10 paragraph 2 enables the reputation of others ... to be protected, and this protection extends to politicians too ... but in such cases the requirements of such protection have to be weighed in relation to the interests of open discussion of political issues.

The Court criticised the Austrian defamation law for placing the burden of proof on the accused to establish the truth of his statements, holding that this could in itself constitute a violation of Article 10:

> A careful distinction needs to be made between facts and value-judgments. The existence of facts can be demonstrated, whereas the truth of value-judgments is not susceptible of proof ... [under Austrian law] journalists in a case such as this cannot escape conviction ... unless they can prove the truth of their statements.... As regards value-judgments this requirement is impossible of fulfilment and it infringes freedom of opinion itself, which is a fundamental part of the right secured by Article 10 of the Convention.

The Court also noted that the government's application of sanctions against a journalist who criticised a political figure:

> [A]mounted to a kind of censure, which would be likely to discourage him from making criticisms ... in the future.... In the context of political debate such a sentence would be likely to deter journalists from contributing to public discussion of issues affecting the life of the community. By the same token, a sanction such as this is liable to hamper the press in performing its task as purveyor of information and public watchdog.

The Court has applied the principles articulated above to a number of cases challenging domestic convictions for defamation, arriving at the same conclusion (see, for example, *Feldek v. Slovakia* (2001)). It has also applied them in several cases in which domestic courts have issued injunctions against the repetition of allegedly harmful or insulting remarks against political or public figures (see, for example, *Dichand and Others v. Austria* (2002) and *Unabhängige Initiative Informationsvielfalt v. Austria* (2002)). In a case in which a domestic injunction had been issued prohibiting the applicant company from publishing a photograph of a politician in connection with a series of articles about his financial situation, the Court found that whether a person or his or her picture was actually known to the public was not important: what was important was whether the person had entered the public arena. In this case, it was clear that the politician had done so, as he had posted his curriculum vitae and photograph on the Austrian Parliament's website (*Krone Verlag GmbH & Co. KG v. Austria* (2002)). Similarly, where a political figure has served a sentence for a criminal offence he cannot then claim that he has been defamed should a journalist reproach him for his conduct in this regard (*Schwabe v. Austria* (1992)). On the other hand, the Court found no violation of Article 10 where a State penalised a journalist who had expressed his opinion about a public figure in a particularly insulting and injurious way, finding that the use of such language was neither justified by public concern nor bore on any matter of general importance (*Tammer v. Estonia* (2001)).

On at least one occasion the European Court has found that political actors may themselves overstep the boundaries of permissible expression in the sense of Article 10 in their criticism of the press. In the case of *Wabl v. Austria* (2000), a newspaper obtained an injunction against a member of parliament who had characterised as "Nazi-journalism" news reports of incidents occurring at a demonstration and in which he was involved. The Court found no violation of Article 10 given the seriousness of the expression, which came close to an accusation of behaviour that constitutes a criminal offence in Austria.

Just as Article 10 of the Convention does not allow special levels of protection for political and public figures in the domestic arena, it also does not allow it for foreign heads of state. In the case of *Colombani and Others v. France* (2002), the applicants had been convicted for "insulting a foreign head of state" for publishing a newspaper article based on a report prepared under the auspices of the European Union identifying Morocco as one of the world's leading drug exporters and questioning the avowed determination of the Moroccan authorities, including King Hassan II, to combat drug trafficking on the territory. The European Court of Human Rights held that for any individual to be immune from criticism solely on the basis of his or her function or status was too broad a privilege to be compatible with Article 10.

The Court has reviewed an increasing number of cases alleging violations of Article 10 where an author, editor or publisher has been convicted for incitement to racial hatred and hostility, incitement to violence, or for speech advocating against the sovereignty or territorial integrity of the State. With very few exceptions, the Court has upheld the right of the individual to express views that the domestic courts had penalised, regularly finding violations of Article 10 where States have prosecuted individuals for expressing views considered to constitute threats to the sovereignty, indivisibility or territorial integrity of the State, as long as the individuals had not called for violence or hatred (see, for example, *Incal v. Turkey* (1998), *Başkaya and Okçuoğlu v. Turkey* (1999) and *Karatas v. Turkey* (1999)). Even should the State assert that a conviction was justifiable as an aspect of the fight against terrorism, the Court has held that this assertion does not permit the State to unduly restrict the right of the public to be informed of controversial views by bringing the weight of the criminal law to bear on the media (*Erdoğdu and Ince v. Turkey* (1999)). The State will find itself on even weaker ground should it permit an executive authority to ban a publication on the basis of the authority's perception that it constitutes a threat to public order, particularly if the work in question has been published and distributed in other States Parties (*Association Ekin v. France* (2001)).

The Court has been similarly unsympathetic to States attempting to embargo open debate on other topics of public concern, finding a violation of Article 10 where a State had prosecuted a journalist for incitement to racial hatred for his reporting on an extremist youth movement (*Jersild v. Denmark* (1994)). In the case of *Lehideux and Isorni v. France* (1998), the applicants had been convicted and found liable for civil damages for publishing an advertisement in a French newspaper defending the actions of Marechal Petain (a Second World War collaborator with the enemy). As the applicant's organisation was registered legally in France for this express purpose, the Court found that penalising it for pursuing its stated aim constituted a violation of Article 10. In contrast to these two cases, the Court found no violation of Article 10 with respect to the criminal conviction of a man who had published a book whose purposes were to deny that the Holocaust had occurred and to rehabilitate Nazism. The Court considered that the denial of crimes against humanity was an acute form of racial defamation and of incitement to racial hatred and that the rewriting of this aspect of history posed a serious threat to public order. It was thus incompatible with democracy and human rights and was intended to achieve objectives prohibited by Article 17 of the Convention (see also Chapter 8 above) (*Garaudy v. France* (2003)).

Some of the most important cases under Article 10 relate to the rights of newspapers to freedom of expression in the context of discussion of matters of general interest to the public, in the non-political as well as the political context. In these cases, the Convention institutions balance very carefully the interests of the press in publishing against those of the State in restricting the public's receipt of information.

The leading case on freedom of the press under Article 10 is the case of *Sunday Times v. the United Kingdom (No. 1)* (1979). In this case, the applicants had prepared for publication a news article outlining the scientific research and testing procedures followed by a pharmaceutical company prior to its marketing of the sedative thalidomide. At the proposed time of publication, it had been considered (through means independent of news coverage) that many babies had suffered from severe birth defects because their mothers had taken the drug during pregnancy. Some of the affected families had negotiated out-of-court settlements with the pharmaceutical company, others were still in the negotiation process, and a few families were in the early stages of litigation. On receiving a copy of the proposed newspaper article, the pharmaceutical company applied for and was granted an injunction against its publication, on the grounds that publication of the article would constitute contempt of court, by interfering with or prejudicing the course of justice in the pending legal proceedings. The European Court of Human Rights accepted that the injunction had been lawful in the sense of the Convention and that it had been issued for a legitimate purpose, to maintain the authority and impartiality of the judiciary. However, the Court held that the United Kingdom Government had failed to establish that the enforcement of the injunction corresponded to a "pressing social need", or was "proportionate to the legitimate aim pursued". The Court held that the public in general had a right to receive information about the matter, even if the facts and issues formed the background to pending litigation. It highlighted several factors as important to its judgment, for example, the breadth and the unqualified restriction of the injunction, the moderate nature of the specific article being enjoined, the length and dormant nature of the legal proceedings and settlement negotiations, and the extensive public debate engaged concerning the subject matter of the article. Thus, the Court established a high level of protection for the press, founding this protection on the presumption that the public interest is best served by ensuring that the broadest body of information is available to the population.

Several States Parties to the Convention have legal prohibitions against the publication of information related to matters that are before the courts. In the case of *Du Roy and Malaurie v. France* (2000), two journalists had been convicted for publishing information concerning applications to join criminal proceedings as a civil party, an offence under a statute establishing a general and absolute prohibition on the publication of such information. The Court found a violation of Article 10, given the absolute nature of the prohibition and the impediment to the right of the press to inform the public about a matter clearly in the public interest, the allegedly fraudulent actions of French political figures in their capacities as directors of a public company managing housing. In contrast, the Court found no violation of Article 10 in a case in which a journalist was convicted for criminal defamation for publishing comments about a trade union dispute, including implications of criminal conduct by previous trade union leaders against whom charges had been dropped (*Constantinescu v. Romania* (2000)).

In the case of *Barthold v. Germany* (1985), a veterinary surgeon had been interviewed by the press about the availability of emergency veterinary services. Several other veterinary surgeons practising in the same region complained to the professional association that the interview constituted "publicity" prohibited by the rules of professional conduct for veterinary surgeons. The association obtained an injunction restraining the applicant from repeating specific statements to the press. In finding a violation of Article 10, the Court noted that the German Government's regulations were "not consonant with freedom of expression" in that they virtually precluded the participation of members of given professions in public debate, and could serve "to hamper the press in the performance of its task of purveyor of information and public watchdog".

Article 10 of the Convention provides protection to private persons as well as journalists and public figures. The Court found a violation of Article 10 in the case of *Marônek v. Slovakia* (2001), in which the applicant had been convicted for defamation for having written an open letter to a newspaper regarding the illegal occupancy of his apartment and soliciting others with the same problem to take joint action on the matter. The Court observed that the issues raised in the letter were a matter of general public interest at the time, given the State's plans to de-nationalise State-owned apartments. It also found a violation in the case of *Bowman v. the United Kingdom* (1998) for the prosecution of an individual for distributing campaign leaflets prior to a general election, in violation of a domestic law prohibiting the expenditure of more than five pounds to promote the election of a candidate during a pre-election period. The Court considered this restriction to be disproportionate, given that the press could take positions on candidates and that political parties were permitted to advertise during the same period.

As alluded to above in connection with the *Jerusalem* case, the Court has found that the extent to which an individual has entered into the public arena or a public debate serves to determine the degree of tolerance that he or she must have for criticism (*Nilsen and Johnsen v. Norway* (1999)). Similarly, in the context of general public debate the Court applies many of the same principles that apply to political debate. For example, it considers that the expression of opinions on matters of public interest must be given broad latitude, often finding State demands that individuals charged with defamation offences must prove the truth of their assertions to be in contra-vention of Article 10. It has found violations in cases in which applicants have been convicted of defamation although the materials on which they relied were produced by or under the auspices of the government (*Bladet Tromsø and Stensaas v. Norway* (1999) or in which the domestic courts failed to review documentation on which allegedly defamatory articles had been based (*Dalban v. Romania* (2000)). Similarly, should a journalist utilise mate-rial formulated by a fellow journalist, he or she cannot be convicted for defa-mation for having failed to conduct independent research into the same matter (*Thoma v. Luxembourg* (2001)).

4. Freedom of expression and publicly available information

Should information be widely available to the public, the Court will normally find a violation of Article 10 if journalists are enjoined from or punished for using such information. The joined cases of *Observer and Guardian v. the United Kingdom* (1991) and *Sunday Times v. the United Kingdom* (*No. 2*) (1991) related to the publication in the two newspapers of information and excerpts from a book published by a retired member of the British security service alleging that the service had conducted certain illegal activities. The Court found that the issuance of a temporary injunction against publication pending the outcome of proceedings against the author in the English courts was compatible with Article 10 as falling within the State's margin of appre-ciation in assessing a threat to national security. On the other hand, the Court found that the continuation of the injunction after the confidentiality of the material had been largely destroyed by the widespread dissemination of the contested information, including the publication and sale of the book in several countries and its unrestricted import into the United Kingdom, constituted a violation of Article 10.

The Court applied its reasoning in these cases to the later case of *Vereniging Weekblad Bluf! v. the Netherlands* (1995) in which the editors of a periodical printed a report about the activities of the internal security service. Although the relevant print run of the periodical was seized and the editors arrested, the staff of the periodical printed a new run and distributed it the following day. The Court found a violation of Article 10. It also found a violation where a news organisation was prohibited from publishing a photograph of a cri-minal suspect who was a public figure, although the relevant domestic law permitted such publication (*News Verlags GmbH and Co.KG v. Austria* (2000)), where two journalists were convicted for publishing information about the financial and tax circumstances of the head of a large company, although the information at issue was widely available through the public tax records (*Fressoz and Roire v. France* (1999)) and where a journalist and environmental activist were convicted for having breached, at a press confe-rence, the confidentiality of a judicial investigation the facts of which were already in the public domain at the time of the press conference (*Weber v. Switzerland* (1990)).

5. Disclosure of journalists' sources

One important aspect of the broad protection afforded to the media in the exercise of their right to freedom of expression is the protection of confidential sources of information that form the basis of much investigative journalism. In the case of *Goodwin v. the United Kingdom* (1996), the Court found a violation of Article 10 where the government imposed not only an injunction against the publication of an article but also an order to disclose the sources of the information contained therein on a journalist reporting on the business practices of a company. Although the Court found that the protection of the rights of the company constituted a legitimate aim, the means chosen to achieve that aim were disproportionate to its achievement. The Court has also found violations of Article 10 where authorities have conducted searches of journalists' homes or offices for the purpose of establishing the identity of or obtaining other information about the journalists' sources, in circumstances in which no suspicion existed that the journalists themselves were involved in any criminal activity (*Roemen and Schmit v. Luxembourg* (2003) and *Ernst and Others v. Belgium* (2003)). In both of these cases, the Court found that the searches undermined the protection of the journalists' sources to an even greater extent than the measures at issue in *Goodwin*.

6. Freedom of expression and respect for the judiciary

Unlike its approach to press criticism of other public figures, the Court has taken a more restrictive view of press or public criticism of the judiciary or officers of the court. In the case of *Barfod v. Denmark* (1989), the applicant had published a newspaper article criticising a judgment upholding the legality of a decision by a local government body. He based his criticism on the grounds that two of the three judges were lay judges employed by the local government, the body that was the defendant in the case. In his article, the applicant expressed the opinion that the two lay judges could be expected to "do their duty", that is to vote in favour of their employer's interests. The government successfully prosecuted the applicant for defamation, although at the same time the domestic courts noted that the lay judges should not have participated in the case. The Court found no violation of Article 10, stating:

> The State's legitimate interest in protecting the reputation of the two lay judges was ... not in conflict with the applicant's interest in being able to participate in free public debate on the question of the structural impartiality of the High Court.

In a case in which a disciplinary penalty had been imposed on a lawyer for his criticism of the judiciary during a press conference, the Court found no violation of Article 10 (*Schöpfer v. Switzerland* (1998)). In contrast, the Court did find a violation of Article 10 in the case of *De Haes and Gijsels v. Belgium* (1997) where a journalist criticised the award of custody of children to a man convicted of incest and child abuse and suggested that the judges making the award had done so on the basis of political bias.

With respect to criticism of public prosecutors and other governmental agents involved in judicial proceedings, the Court found a violation of Article 10 where a defence lawyer was convicted of defamation for issuing a public statement in which she used strong language in accusing the prosecutor in a case in which they represented opposite sides of improper conduct. The Court found a violation of Article 10 on the grounds that a prosecutor is entitled to less protection than a judge, noting also that the criticism at issue had been directed at the prosecution's strategy and performance in the case, and had not amounted to a personal insult. The Court further found that the threat of *ex post facto* review of counsel's criticism of another party was difficult to reconcile with a defence counsel's duty to defend his or her client's interests (*Nikula v. Finland* (2002)). It came to the same conclusion where disciplinary action had been taken against a lawyer on account of statements made in his professional capacity during court proceedings (*Steur v. the Netherlands* (2003)). The Court also found a violation of Article 10 where a journalist was convicted for having accused a prosecutor of being a militant member of a political party, considering that the strong political bias of a member of the judiciary is a major concern of public interest. However, it found no violation for his conviction for alleging that the prosecutor was participating in a strategy to take control over many public prosecutors' offices, as this allegation was unsupported by any facts (*Perna v. Italy* (2001)).

With respect to fostering respect for judicial processes, the Court found no violation of Article 10 where a journalist had been convicted for publishing an article considered capable of influencing the outcome of criminal proceedings, even though the defendant was a former Vice-Chancellor and Finance Minister. In the article at issue, the journalist had both assessed evidence and expressed the opinion that the defendant was guilty of the alleged offence (*Worm v. Austria* (1997)).

7. Positive obligations of the State under Article 10

In recent years, the Court has established the principle that a State may have a positive obligation to protect journalists and news publishers from intimidation, harassment or violence. In the case of *Özgür Gündem v. Turkey* (2000), for example, the Court found a violation of Article 10 where the government failed to provide protection for a newspaper that had been subject to terrorist attacks. The Court stated that freedom of expression must be guaranteed in part by the State's providing a secure environment for its exercise. Where journalists and distributors of a newspaper had been injured, ill-treated or even killed and where the government had not responded to requests for protection against and investigation of these crimes, the Court also found a violation of Article 10 (*Özgür Gündem*).

In the case of *Fuentes Bobo v. Spain* (2000), the Court held that Article 10 applies in the context of the relations of private broadcasters with their employees. In this case, a television producer whose programme was cancelled and who was not offered an alternative job criticised the management of the broadcasting company for which he worked. He was first disciplined and later dismissed from his position with the company. In finding a violation of Article 10, the Court held that the State has an affirmative obligation to protect the right to freedom of expression in the context of such relationships.

The Court has found that the right to freedom of expression does not create an automatic right of access to a particular forum for the exercise of that right, finding no violation of Article 10 where owners of a privately owned shopping mall refused to permit the applicants to distribute leaflets, collect signatures for a petition or otherwise conduct an information campaign regarding a matter of local public interest. The Court did note, however, that if no other means existed for the communication of such views, so that the essence of the protected right was destroyed, a positive obligation could arise for the State to regulate property rights to guarantee such access (*Appleby v. the United Kingdom* (2003)).

8. Licensing of broadcasting facilities

Article 10 of the European Convention on Human Rights explicitly permits the State to regulate the broadcasting media, stating in paragraph 1: "This Article shall not prevent States from requiring the licensing of broadcasting, television, or cinema enterprises." The Court has held that in spite of the wording of this sentence, states must be able to justify licensing requirements or practices in light of the purpose of the Article as a whole. The applicants in the cases of *Informationsverein Lentia and Others v. Austria* (1993) and *Radio ABC v. Austria* (1997) contested the government's denial of broadcasting licences to them and thus effectively also challenged the continuing monopoly of the Austrian Broadcasting Corporation. The Court found a violation of Article 10 in both cases, noting that state monopolies over broadcasting imposed the greatest restrictions on pluralism in expression and thus could only be justified where there was a pressing social need. Given the extent of technological progress in the area of broadcasting and the opening of a large number of broadcasting frequencies, no such need could be advanced to impose a blanket prohibition on the operation of private broadcast media.

The Court has considered a few cases raising the issue of whether the right to broadcast implies the right to be free from governmental interference with reception of broadcasts. In the case of *Groppera Radio AG and Others v. Switzerland* (1990), a Swiss radio company with interests in an Italian subsidiary and several individuals affiliated with the companies complained that a Swiss prohibition against a Swiss cable company's retransmitting radio programmes broadcast by the applicants from Italy constituted a violation of Article 10. The Court noted that licensing of broadcasting facilities was permitted under Article 10(1), but that the State could only exercise its licensing power in the context of the Article as a whole. It found that the domestic law was both foreseeable and accessible and that the restriction itself responded to a legitimate aim. The Court thus held that there was no violation of Article 10, as the Swiss Government had chosen a means of restriction that "could well appear necessary in order to prevent evasion of the law [and] was not a form of censorship".

In the case of *Autronic AG v. Switzerland* (1990), a Swiss telecommunications company was refused governmental authorisation to receive uncoded television programmes from a Soviet satellite, in the absence of Soviet consent. The Court first noted that reception of television programmes comes within the scope of the right to receive information under Article 10(1). It also noted that the relevant Swiss legislation was sufficiently accessible to the specialised public for which it was intended. In finding a violation of Article 10, however, the Court held that because the broadcasts at issue were intended for the general use of the public and because the Swiss Government accepted that there was no risk of obtaining secret information through receipt of the broadcasts, the restrictions imposed were not necessary in a democratic society as they exceeded the State's margin of appreciation.

In the case of *Demuth v. Switzerland* (2002), the Court clarified that Article 10 permits States to regulate broadcasting on their territories not only with respect to technical aspects, but also to other considerations as well, for example the purpose, functions and contents of programmes in light of the need for quality control and balance in programming. In this case, the applicant complained about the refusal of the Swiss authorities to grant him a licence to broadcast a television programme about cars via cable television. In finding no violation of Article 10, the Court noted that the negative decision of the Swiss Federal Broadcasting Council indicated that it would consider granting the licence if the contents of the planned programme contributed to the aims set out in the relevant domestic legislation.

9. Commercial free speech

The Court has reviewed very few cases claiming violations of Article 10 with respect to freedom of expression in the commercial context. In the case of *markt intern Verlag GmbH and Klaus Beermann v. Germany* (1989), the publishers of a trade publication serving small and medium-sized companies published an article criticising the conduct of a large firm operating in the same line of business with respect to a single incident and solicited further information from its readers about similar incidents or practices. The competent domestic court found the applicants to have engaged in unfair business practices and ordered them to refrain from further publication of the statements at issue. In finding no violation of Article 10, the Court noted that on being informed about the allegations against it the company had immediately launched an investigation into the matter, and observed that publishing information about the incident under the circumstances was premature and could lead to disproportionate harm to the company. In the case of *Jacubowski v. Germany* (1994), the Court found no violation of Article 10 where the government prosecuted a person who had been dismissed from his job, had set up his own business in the same line of work and had thereafter distributed newspaper clippings and other materials critical of his former employer to professional colleagues.

The Court distinguished between purely commercial speech and speech that is connected with commerce but is de facto speech on a matter of public interest in the case of *Hertel v. Switzerland* (1998). In this case, the State had prohibited a private individual from stating that consumption of food prepared in microwave ovens was dangerous to human health, after he had published an article on the subject. The Court found a violation of Article 10 on the grounds that the expression of this type of opinion did not fall within the purview of the domestic law on unfair competition, under which the prohibition had been issued.

With respect to access to broadcast media for those wishing to broadcast paid advertisements, the Court found a violation of Article 10 where no means existed through which an individual could challenge a refusal to broadcast an advertisement and where the medium at issue was the only one with nationwide coverage (*VgT Verein gegen Tierfabriken v. Switzerland* (2001)). However, it found no violation where the State refused to permit paid advertising by religious groups, finding that this restriction fell within the State's margin of appreciation, particularly given the existence of alternative means for expression (*Murphy v. Ireland* (2003)).

10. Freedom of artistic expression

As noted at the beginning of this chapter, the European Court of Human Rights has extended a wide margin of appreciation to States to restrict the freedom of expression of artistic ideas. In a case in which the "protection of morals" clause was at issue, the applicants complained that the Swiss Government's confiscation of several sexually explicit paintings and its fining of the artist for publishing obscene materials constituted a violation of Article 10 (*Müller and Others v. Switzerland* (1988)). In finding the State's actions justified under the second paragraph, the Court accepted that States have a wide margin of appreciation in determining what is "necessary" for the "protection of morals". However, in delivering its judgment, the Court noted that the term "expression" under Article 10 encompasses artistic expression, "which affords the opportunity to take part in the public exchange of cultural, political and social information and ideas of all kinds". The Court has also deferred to the States where the religious feelings of parts of the population might be offended by the exercise of artistic expression. In the cases of *Otto-Preminger-Institut v. Austria* (1994) and *Wingrove v. the United Kingdom* (1996), the Court found no violation of Article 10 where the respective governments prohibited the exhibition of films that presented irreverent images and interpretations of certain Christian figures and practices.

In recent years, the Court has considered a number of cases where authorities have prohibited the publication of literary works on the grounds that the literature in question expressed prohibited political views. As in other cases in which purely public interest or political expression was at issue, the Court has found violations of Article 10 in most of these cases, stressing such factors as the limited impact of literary works on national security, the failure of the State to show that negative views of the majority of the population could be equated with incitement to violence, armed resistance or an uprising, and the severity of penalties imposed (see, for example, *Karatas v. Turkey* (1999) and *Arslan v. Turkey* (1999)).

11. Duties and responsibilities of individuals under Article 10

Under Article 10(1), "everyone" has the right to freedom of expression, including the freedom to receive and impart information and ideas. Under Article 10(2), however, an individual may exercise these freedoms only in light of his or her duties and responsibilities. As should be clear from the case-law discussed throughout this chapter, in general the European Court of Human Rights will favour members of the press and private individuals over public and political figures. At the same time, it is worth noting that it has accepted that a State may restrict the freedom of political expression of governmental authorities or agents, finding no violation of Article 10 in the restriction of political activities of local governmental officers in designated posts (*Ahmed and Others v. the United Kingdom* (1998)) or of members of the armed forces, police and security services (*Rekvényi v. Hungary* (1999)). With respect to non-political speech and activities, however, the Court will determine on a case-by-case basis whether a restriction on particular governmental authorities or agents is acceptable under Article 10. The Court has reviewed several cases relating to the freedom of expression of members of the armed forces in this context, finding no violation of Article 10 in the case of *Engel and Others v. the Netherlands* (1976), in which the applicants complained of disciplinary action taken against them for the publication and distribution of a paper criticising certain senior officers. The Court arrived at the opposite view in the case of *Vereinigung demokratischer Soldaten Österreichs and Gubi v. Austria* (1994), challenging the refusal to permit the distribution to military conscripts of a publication critical of the administration of the military. In finding a violation of Article 10, the Court noted that the publication at issue did not recommend any course of action that would threaten military discipline and did not overstep "the bounds of what is permissible in the context of a mere discussion of ideas, which must be tolerated in the army of a democratic State just as it must be in the society that such an army serves". The Court also found a violation of Article 10 where an individual was disciplined for sending a letter criticising the army to his commanding officer: the letter was neither published nor disseminated (*Grigoriades v. Greece* (1997)).

The Court has addressed the issue of dismissal or denial of access to employment of those exercising their rights to freedom of expression under Article 10, changing its views on the matter over the course of time. In the cases of *Kosiek v. Germany* (1986) and *Glasenapp v. Germany* (1986), the Court reviewed the Federal Republic of Germany's doctrine of *Berufsverbot,* the requirement that all civil servants must swear allegiance to the German Constitution and its values. Ms Glasenapp had expressed certain views sympathetic to those of the far political left; Mr Kosiek to the far political right.

In both these cases, the government declined to confer permanent civil service status on the applicants, each of whom held a probationary appointment as a school teacher. In finding the government's actions acceptable under Article 10, the Court noted in both cases that the European Convention on Human Rights does not guarantee access to civil service appointments. It then stated that the government authorities took account of the applicants' opinions, attitudes and activities only to determine whether they met the "necessary personal qualifications for the post in question". It is worth noting in this context, however, that the International Labour Organization conducted a Commission of Inquiry of these and similar cases and found the Federal Republic of Germany in violation of its obligations under the ILO Discrimination (Employment and Occupation) Convention, 1958 (No. 111). In 1995 the Court arrived at the opposite conclusion in the case of *Vogt v. Germany,* in which it held that the dismissal of a language teacher from her position on the grounds of her membership in the German Communist Party constituted a violation of Article 10. The Court also found a violation in a case in which the President of the Administrative Court of Liechtenstein made a public statement about the competence of the Constitutional Court to rule on the interpretation of the constitution in the event of a conflict between the Prince of Liechtenstein and the Diet. The Prince informed the applicant that he would never be nominated to any public position, due to his opinions on this matter, and subsequently refused to re-appoint him when his position was up for renewal (*Wille v. Liechtenstein* (1999)).

12. The right to receive and to impart information

The Court has examined an individual's right under Article 10 to receive information relating to governmental decisions on civil service employment. In the case of *Leander v. Sweden* (1987), the Swedish Government had denied the applicant a public appointment on the grounds that he did not meet the security requirements of the post. He requested information about the contents of the government's file on him in order to clarify or rebut any inaccuracies: the government denied the request. The Court upheld this refusal in part on the grounds that access to public employment is not a protected right under the European Convention on Human Rights and in part on the grounds that the "freedom to receive information" clause of Article 10:

> Basically prohibits a Government from restricting a person from receiving information that others wish or may be willing to impart to him. Article 10 does not, in circumstances such as those of the present case, confer on the individual a right of access to a register containing information on his personal position, nor does it embody an obligation on the Government to impart such information to the individual.

In this light, the Court found a violation of the right to receive information where there was no basis in domestic law for the denial of access to reading materials, radio and television to an individual in psychiatric detention (*Herczegfalvy v. Austria* (1992)).

Both the right to impart and the right to have access to information about the availability of abortions abroad were at issue in the case of *Open Door and Dublin Well Woman v. Ireland* (1992). This case challenged the issuing of an injunction against two companies prohibiting them from providing such information to pregnant women as part of their counselling services. In finding a violation of Article 10, the Court took note of a number of factors, including the sweeping nature of the injunction, the availability of such information from other sources and the lack of any prohibition against women actually seeking abortions abroad.

Finally, it is worth noting that the Court found a violation of Article 10 where the Turkish authorities instituted excessive measures of censorship of school books destined for use by Greek Cypriot primary school students in northern Cyprus (*Cyprus v. Turkey* (2001)).

Chapter 12 – Freedom of assembly and association: Article 11

Article 11

> 1.   Everyone has the right to freedom of peaceful assembly and to freedom of association with others, including the right to form and to join trade unions for the protection of his interests.
>
> 2.   No restrictions shall be placed on the exercise of these rights other than such as are prescribed by law and are necessary in a democratic society in the interests of national security or public safety, for the prevention of disorder or crime, for the protection of health or morals or for the protection of the rights and freedoms of others. This Article shall not prevent the imposition of lawful restrictions on the exercise of these rights by members of the armed forces, of the police or of the administration of the State.

The rights guaranteed by Article 11 are linked to, or justified by, the political and social values of a democratic society. To a great extent, the rights guaranteed under Article 11 represent an extension and expansion of the rights to freedom of thought, conscience and religion under Article 9 and the right to freedom of expression under Article 10. Indeed, Article 9 implicitly allows the rights of assembly and association in its guarantee of the freedom to manifest religion or belief "in community with others and in public or private". Similarly, the Convention institutions consistently maintain that the rights guaranteed under Article 10 (freedom of expression) touch on group activities such as demonstrations. Although it considers Article 11 to be *lex specialis* in these cases, the Court has regard to Article 10 when interpreting freedom of assembly and association cases under Article 11 (*Ezelin v. France* (1991) and *Socialist Party and Others v. Turkey* (1998)).

1. The right of peaceful assembly

The European Court of Human Rights has broadly interpreted the right to freedom of assembly to cover both private meetings and meetings in public thoroughfares as well as static meetings and public processions. It has also held that the right can be exercised by both individuals and those organising an assembly (*Djavit An v. Turkey* (2003)). In the light of this broad interpretation, the Court has held that the State cannot place arbitrary restrictions on the right of peaceful assembly by refusing to issue necessary permits to organise or participate in such assemblies, by failing to provide police protection to demonstrators or by otherwise not meeting its positive obligations to secure the right. In balancing the legitimate interests of the State under Article 11 with the rights of the individual or association, the Court will also take into consideration alternative means of controlling or penalising unacceptable conduct should it transpire (see, for example, *Stankov and the United Macedonian Organisation Ilinden v. Bulgaria* (2001)).

The Court has found a violation of the right of peaceful assembly where the State refused to permit an individual to cross from northern to southern Cyprus to attend bi-communal meetings (*Djavit An v. Turkey* (2003)). The applicant in this case was the "Turkish Cypriot Co-ordinator" of the "Movement for an Independent and Federal Cyprus", an unregistered association of Turkish and Greek Cypriots whose purpose was to develop close relations between the two communities. The Court noted that there seemed to be no law that regulated the issuance of permits to Turkish Cypriots living in northern Cyprus to cross the "green line" into southern Cyprus in order to assemble peacefully with Greek Cypriots. It thus found that the manner in which restrictions were imposed on the applicant's exercise of his freedom of assembly was not "prescribed by law" within the meaning of paragraph 2 of Article 11 of the Convention.

The Court considered the right to peaceful assembly of an unregistered association in the case of *Stankov and the United Macedonian Organisation Ilinden v. Bulgaria* (2001). In this case, the State had refused to register an association whose stated goals, *inter alia,* were to unite all Macedonians in Bulgaria and to achieve the recognition of the Macedonian minority. The organisation had also declared that it would not infringe the territorial integrity of the State nor use violent or unlawful means in pursuit of its goals. Subsequently, the authorities refused several requests to allow the association to hold commemorative meetings, basing their decisions in part on the refusal to register the association and the alleged likelihood that separatist declarations would be made at any such meetings. The European Court of Human Rights noted that even if a group of persons calls for autonomy, requests secession of part of the country's territory or otherwise demands fundamental constitutional and territorial changes, such views could not automatically justify a prohibition of its assemblies. The Court found a violation of Article 11, enjoining the national authorities in particular to exercise particular vigilance to ensure that national public opinion is not protected at the expense of the assertion of minority views, however unpopular they may be.

In the case of *Plattform "Ärzte für das Leben" v. Austria* (1988), the Court examined the State's affirmative obligation to provide protection to groups exercising the right of peaceful assembly. In this case, the Government had given permission for an anti-abortion demonstration in one location: the applicant organisation then requested and was granted a change in location to one less suitable to crowd control. The authorities notified the organisers of the demonstration that the police might not be able to afford adequate protection against counter-demonstrations, which did in fact occur. Similar difficulties arose at a second demonstration. The applicant organisation complained that the Government had violated Article 11 by failing to take adequate measures to ensure that the demonstrations occurred without any trouble.

The Court held that Austria had an obligation to provide protection to groups exercising the right of peaceful assembly:

> A demonstration may annoy or give offence to persons opposed to the ideas or claims that it is seeking to promote. The participants must, however, be able to

hold the demonstration without having to fear that they will be subjected to physical violence by their opponents; such a fear would be liable to deter associations or other groups supporting common ideas or interests from openly expressing their opinions on highly controversial issues affecting the community. In a democracy the right to counter-demonstrate cannot extend to inhibiting the exercise of the right to demonstrate. (paragraph 32)

The Court does, however, allow States a broad margin of appreciation in this area, as well as considering that a State's obligation is one of conduct and not results. In the instant case, the Court held that the Austrian authorities had taken all reasonable and appropriate measures to protect the demonstrators, and that there was thus no violation of Article 11.

2. The right to association

The Convention institutions have made clear that an association is more formal and organised than an assembly, presupposing a voluntary grouping for the pursuit of a common goal.

The "voluntary nature" criterion is of particular importance to those cases addressing the "negative" approach to rights under Article 11, in other words the right not to join an association or trade union. The Court addressed this issue in its judgment in the case of *Young, James and Webster v. the United Kingdom* (1981), in which the applicants claimed that an agreement concluded between British Rail and certain railwaymen's trade unions, conditioning employment on membership in one of these unions, violated the freedom of association provision under Article 11. The Court agreed, holding that the applicants could not be compelled to join a trade union in order to keep their jobs:

> The right to form and to join trade unions is a special aspect of freedom of association ... the notion of a freedom implies some measure of freedom of choice as to its exercise....

> It does not follow that the negative aspect of a person's freedom of association falls completely outside the ambit of Article 11 and that each and every compulsion to join a particular trade union is compatible with the intention of that provision. To construe Article 11 as permitting every kind of compulsion in the field of trade union membership would strike at the very substance of the freedom it is designed to guarantee. (paragraph 52)

It is important to note, however, that the Court *in obiter dicta* noted that such "closed shop" agreements did not necessarily automatically violate Article 11. The Court held instead that in this particular instance the applicants' rights under Article 11 had been violated, as their continued employment was at issue. The Court also found a violation of Article 11 in the case of *Sigurdur A. Sigurjónsson v. Iceland* (1993). In this case, a taxi driver was granted a licence on the condition that he join the Automobile Association. He did so, but subsequently let his membership expire, at which point the Association revoked his taxicab licence. Three years later, the Icelandic Parliament passed a law requiring all taxi drivers to be members of the

Association. The Court found that the legal imposition of such a membership obligation was disproportionate to the aim pursued.

The voluntary nature of the freedom of association was also at issue in the case of *Chassagnou and Others v. France* (1999). In this case, the applicants owned land in an area where the applicable law required all landowners whose holdings were smaller than a certain area to become a member of the relevant "inter-municipality hunters' association" and to transfer to it hunting rights over their land. Only holders of larger properties were entitled to object to the transfer of those rights. In finding a violation of Article 11, the Court noted that the right to hunt, which was not a right guaranteed under the Convention could not be balanced against the freedom of association, which is so guaranteed. The Court also stressed that the compulsion by law to join an association that was fundamentally contrary to someone's convictions and to thereby oblige him or her to act against those convictions did not achieve a fair balance between conflicting interests and could not be considered proportionate to the aim pursued.

The Court has held that an individual can be compelled to join certain organisations, on the grounds that they are not "associations" in the Article 11 sense. In the case of *Le Compte, Van Leuven and De Meyere v. Belgium* (1981), for example, the Convention institutions found that the applicant doctors could be compelled to join the Belgian Medical Association, on the grounds that this body was not an "association" within the meaning of Article 11, as it fulfilled public law functions, for example the monitoring of its members' professional conduct.

3. Banning or dissolution of associations

As alluded to above, the Court generally views with disfavour any governmental restriction on rights guaranteed under Article 11 prior to their exercise. In the case of *Sidiropoulos and Others v. Greece* (1998), the Government had refused to register an association whose aims were the preservation of Macedonian culture and folklore and the protection of the natural and cultural environment of the region in which they were located. The grounds advanced as the justification for refusing to register the association were the suspicion that the association wished to undermine the territorial integrity of the country. In finding a violation of Article 11, the Court noted that the refusal to register the association had deprived the applicants of any possibility of jointly or individually pursuing the aims they had laid down in the memorandum of association and thus of exercising the right in question. The Court considered that the aims of the association were both clear and legitimate under several European human rights standard setting documents. It also noted that Greek law did not lay down an effective system of preventive review for the setting up of non-profit-making associations, vesting the courts with powers to order the dissolution of an association if, after its registration, it pursued an aim different from the one laid down in its memorandum of association. In the instant case, registration had been disallowed prior to the association's taking any action at all, the court having based its decision on the suspicion as to the true intentions of the association's founders and the activities it might have engaged in once it had begun to function.

The disfavour with which the Court generally views prior restraints on the freedom of association through a government's refusing to register an association or prohibiting it from peacefully pursuing the goals for whose achievement it was established extends also to such governmental actions with respect to political parties. However, in both contexts, the Court has held that it may be permissible for a State to dissolve an association (political or otherwise) for engaging in activities incompatible with the aims of its memorandum of association. The Court has been called upon to review a number of cases in which political parties have been dissolved or banned. With few exceptions, the Court has found violations of Article 11, declining to review complaints of violations of Article 10 or Article 3 of Protocol No. 1.

As with respect to the freedom of assembly cases discussed above, domestic decisions to ban political parties have often been based on public speeches or other exercises of freedom of expression by the leaders of the party being banned. The Court has consistently held that even very strong assertions of political claims or the presentation of political programmes aimed at the establishment of different political organisational structures within a country cannot be considered as justifying a ban on a political party, as long as the party does not incite violence against the government or individuals not subscribing to the party's views. The Court has found violations of the right to freedom of association in several cases in which the political parties that had been banned had stayed well within the parameters of democratic debate, expressing their views forcefully, but not overstepping the line of incitement (see, for example, *Socialist Party and Others v. Turkey* (1998)). The Court made even stronger pronouncements in the case of *United Communist Party of Turkey and Others v. Turkey* (1998), finding a violation of Article 11 where the party had been dissolved even before it had been able to start its activities, solely on the basis of its constitution and programme, and, in part, on its inclusion of the term "communist" in its name. In both of the preceding judgments, the Court also noted that the programme of a political party or the statements of its leaders may conceal objectives and intentions different from those they proclaim. However, to verify that they do not, the content of the programme or statements must be compared with the actions of the party and its leaders and the positions they defend taken as a whole. Where leaders of associations have been prosecuted, the Court also places weight on the outcome of those criminal cases (*Yazar and Others v. Turkey* (2002) (no party leaders had been convicted of any offences that were cited as grounds for dissolving a political party)).

In contrast to cases in which the Court found a violation of Article 11 in the banning of a political party, the Court found it acceptable for a State to do so where the platform of the party did not conform with the values protected under the European Convention on Human Rights. In the case of *Refah Partisi (the Welfare Party) and Others v. Turkey* (2003), the Court upheld the Government's action in this regard on the grounds that the party wished to introduce Sharia law and a theocratic regime in Turkey. The Court found sharia to diverge from values protected under the Convention, particularly with regard to criminal law and procedure and the legal status of women. The Court considered that where the leaders of an association (or political party) advance a policy which aims at the destruction of democracy, and which flouts rights and freedoms recognised in a democracy, that association cannot lay claim to the Convention's protection against the imposition of penalties or even against preventive measures.

4. Limitations on the protection of trade unions

The European Court of Human Rights does not consider that the right to form and join trade unions guaranteed under Article 11 encompasses a right for trade unions to enjoy a particular level of engagement with employers. The Court stated its position in the cases of *National Union of Belgian Police v. Belgium* (1975) and *Swedish Engine Drivers' Union v. Sweden* (1976), in which it found no interference with the rights guaranteed under the first paragraph of Article 11. In both these cases, the Court noted that a diminishment in the usefulness of trade union membership was brought about by the State's general policy of restricting the number of organisations with which collective agreements were to be concluded and that the policy in itself was not incompatible with trade union freedom. Finally, the Court has held that Article 11 does not protect the right to strike, allowing the State to choose other means by which to safeguard a union's protection of the occupational interests of its members (*Schmidt and Dahlström v. Sweden* (1976)).

In *Wilson & The National Union of Journalists, Palmer, Wyeth & The National Union of Rail, Maritime & Transport Workers, Doolan and Others v. the United Kingdom* (2002), the applicants (individuals and trade unions to which they belonged) complained of a violation of their rights under Article 11 where their private employers had offered individuals significant wage increases and benefits packages under personal contracts which also required those signing the contracts to relinquish all rights to trade union recognition and representation. The applicants refused to sign the contracts, as a result of which their salaries remained at a lower level than those of employees who had accepted personal contracts. The employers subsequently de-recognised the applicant trade unions. The Court found a violation, holding that the State had a positive obligation to ensure that private, as well as public, employers complied with the requirements of Article 11.

> In the present case ... [the] law permitted employers to treat less favourably employees who were not prepared to renounce a freedom that was an essential feature of union membership. Such conduct constituted a disincentive or restraint on the use by employees of union membership to protect their interests.... [D]omestic law did not prohibit the employer from offering an inducement to employees who relinquished the right to union representation, even if the aim and outcome of the exercise was to bring an end to collective bargaining and thus substantially to reduce the authority of the union, as long as the employer did not act with the purpose of preventing or deterring the individual employee simply from being a member of a trade union.

[I]t was ... possible for an employer effectively to undermine or frustrate a trade union's ability to strive for the protection of its members' interests. The Court ... considers that, by permitting employers to use financial incentives to induce employees to surrender important union rights, the respondent State has failed in its positive obligation to secure the enjoyment of the rights under Article 11 of the Convention. This failure amounted to a violation of Article 11, as regards both the applicant trade unions and the individual applicants. (paragraphs 47 and 48)

At the same time, however, the Court also reaffirmed its previous holdings that Article 11 does not secure any particular treatment of trade unions and their members. Nor does it require an employer to recognise a particular trade union for collective bargaining or other purposes, where the domestic law does not establish such obligations.

5. Unique aspects of the restricting provisions of Article 11

Unlike other similarly structured Articles of the Convention, Article 11 contains a provision in paragraph 2 that gives the High Contracting Parties to the Convention power to restrict the exercise of rights guaranteed under paragraph 1 with respect to members of the armed forces, the police or civil servants. In the case of *Rekvényi v. Hungary* (1999), the Court found no violation of Article 10 or 11 where the constitution prohibited police officers from engaging in political activities and joining political parties.

Although not specifically mentioned in the list of governmental employees whose freedom of association a State can legitimately restrict, judges have challenged the placement of such restrictions on them. In *N.F. v. Italy* (2001), the applicant was a judge who had voluntarily relinquished his membership in the Freemasons one year prior to the issuance of a Judicial Service Commission's Directive that membership in certain associations was incompatible with the office of a judge. He was later disciplined for his membership of the association. The European Court of Human Rights found the wording of the directive sufficiently unclear as to fail to meet the standards for lawfulness in the sense of the Convention. A Masonic association of several lodges also brought a claim under Article 11, challenging a regional law that anyone appointed to public office was required to declare that they were not Freemasons (*Grande Oriente d'Italia di Palazzo Giustiniani v. Italy* (2001)). The Court found violations of Article 11 in both of these cases.

Chapter 13 – The right to peaceful enjoyment of possessions: Article 1 of Protocol No. 1

Protocol No. 1 – Article 1

> Every natural or legal person is entitled to the peaceful enjoyment of his or her possessions. No one shall be deprived of his possessions except in the public interest and subject to the conditions provided for by law and by the general principles of international law.
>
> The preceding provisions shall not, however, in any way impair the right of a State to enforce such laws as it deems necessary to control the use of property in accordance with the general interest or to secure the payment of taxes or other contributions or penalties.

Article 1 of Protocol No. 1 to the Convention guarantees the right to peaceful enjoyment of possessions, commonly referred to as the right to property. As with most of the other substantive rights guaranteed by the Convention, States may restrict the exercise of the right to property. It may deprive an individual of his or her possessions "in the public interest and subject to the conditions provided for by law", and it may also "enforce such laws as it deems necessary to control the use of property in accordance with the general interest" or to secure the payment of various fines, taxes and so forth. Thus, the State enjoys a wider margin of appreciation under this Article than it does under other Articles of the Convention that permit restrictions on the enjoyment of rights only if such restrictions are "necessary in a democratic society". It is worth noting that the Court interprets the term "legal persons" broadly.

1. The nature of "possessions" under Article 1 of Protocol No. 1

The Court has reviewed a number of cases in which it has had to delineate the nature of "possessions" under Article 1 of Protocol No. 1. In addition to the common sense interpretation of the term to comprise immovable and movable property, the Court has held that the term "possessions" extends to any "vested rights" an individual may establish, including such private law assets as the right to conclude tenancy agreements (*Mellacher and Others v. Austria* (1989)) or shares or monetary claims based on contracts or torts (*Stran Greek Refineries and Stratis Andreadis v. Greece* (1994)). It also encompasses accrued rights in pension or social security systems (*Vasilopoulou v. Greece* (2002)), a "legitimate expectation" that one will be able to develop a property in accordance with a duly registered development plan (*Pine Valley Developments Ltd. and Others v. Ireland* (1991)), a legal claim of material value (*S.A. Dangeville v. France* (2002)), licences issued in conjunction with the operation of a business (*Tre Traktörer Aktiebolag v. Sweden* (1989)), goodwill engendered through the conduct of professional relationships (*Van Marle and Others v. the Netherlands* (1986)) and compensation claims for expropriated property (discussed below).

Under the Convention, no possession exists until such time as one can perfect a claim to the property at issue. In other words, the right to property does not encompass the right to acquire property. Thus, in the case of *Marckx v. Belgium* (1979) (discussed elsewhere under Articles 8 and 14), the Court held that a mother who was denied the right to will property to her daughter suffered a violation of her rights under Article 1 of Protocol No. 1, but the daughter herself did not, as the expectation of acquiring property was not protected under the Article; and in the case of *Van der Mussele v. Belgium* (1983) (discussed elsewhere under Articles 4 and 14), the Court held that the requirement that a lawyer provide certain services for free did not deprive him of existing possessions, and thus there was no violation of Article 1 of Protocol No. 1. The Court has also held that this provision cannot be interpreted as imposing any restrictions on the Contracting States' freedom to choose conditions under which they accept to restore property which had been transferred to them before they ratified the Convention (*Jantner v. Slovakia* (2003)). However, should it choose to do so, the State must comply with the requirements of Article 1 of Protocol No. 1. In the case of *Brumărescu v. Romania* (1999) and a number of similar cases, the Court found a violation of this provision where the Government refused to return previously nationalised property in spite of the existence of final and binding judgments calling for this course of action. (In these cases, the Court often has found violations of the right to a court guaranteed under Article 6 of the Convention in addition to violations of Article 1 of Protocol No. 1.)

2. "Peaceful enjoyment" of possessions

In their interpretation of the phrase "peaceful enjoyment", the Court has often found itself distinguishing between the notions of deprivation of property and control of its use. For example, in the leading case of *Sporrong and Lönnroth v. Sweden* (1982), the applicants claimed that a Stockholm City Ordinance that authorised the city to expropriate any property it wished, on almost unlimited grounds, violated their right to property under Article 1 of Protocol No. 1. The Court held that although the expropriations at issue technically left the owners the right to use and dispose of their property, in practical terms their possibilities to do so were so drastically reduced that the operation of the Swedish law in fact violated their right to peaceful enjoyment of their possessions. It arrived at a similar conclusion in the case of *Belvedere Alberghiera S.r.l. v. Italy* (2000) where the State expropriated property under an expedited procedure for road-building works, the pursuit of which rendered it impossible for the property to be returned to the owner even after the taking of the property was found to be unlawful.

In its review of the *Sporrong and Lönnroth* case, the Court reiterated its position that the Convention as a whole demands that a balance be struck between the interests of the community and the fundamental rights of the individual. The Court elaborated its views in this regard in the cases of *Lithgow and Others v. the United Kingdom* (1986) and *James and Others v. the United Kingdom* (1986). In the latter case, the applicants contested the operation of a British statute that permitted certain long-term tenants of given residential properties the right to purchase the landlord's interest in the property, in some instances at less than the market value at the time of the transaction. In finding no violation of the right to property, the Court stated:

> [T]he notion of "public interest" is necessarily extensive.... The Court, finding it natural that the margin of appreciation available to the legislature in implementing social and economic policies should be a wide one, will respect the legislature's judgment as to what is "in the public interest" unless that judgment be manifestly without reasonable foundation....

> [A] taking of property affected in pursuance of legitimate social, economic or other policies may be "in the public interest", even if the community at large has no direct use or enjoyment of the property taken.

The French Government exceeded its margin of appreciation with respect to the "public interest" in ensuring the payment of taxes in the case of *Hentrich v. France* (1994). In this case, regional authorities had exercised their right to pre-empt a private property transaction under a statute that afforded broad discretion for them to do so but failed to afford the individual property owner adequate procedural safeguards. The Court found the State's arrogation of absolute power to substitute itself for any purchaser of real property with the sole alleged aim of deterring others from evading taxes placed a disproportionate burden on the individual. There was therefore a violation of Article 1 of Protocol No. 1. Pre-emption was also at issue in the case of *Beyeler v. Italy* (2000), with the same result. In this case, the Italian Government had waited for several years before exercising its right of pre-emption over a valuable work of art, raising questions about the lawfulness of an action to which no time limit apparently applied. It had also compensated the applicant for the taking of his property with an amount that was much less than its market value at the time of the final decision. Although the Court considered that the preservation of artistic works was unquestionably in the public interest, it nevertheless found that the Government had unjustly enriched itself at the expense of the applicant.

Arbitrariness was at issue in the cases of *Katikaridis and Others v. Greece* (1996) and *Tsomtsos and Others v. Greece* (1996). These cases involved the expropriation of property for the purpose of building a highway, coupled with the application of a statute establishing an irrebuttable presumption that the benefits derived from the road improvements amounted to adequate compensation to the individuals affected. The Court held that the inflexibility of the system of awarding compensation and in particular the impossibility of having a judicial determination of real losses accruing as a result of the expropriation constituted a violation of Article 1 of Protocol No. 1. In the case of *Chassagnou v. France* (1999), the Court similarly found a violation of Article 1 of Protocol No. 1 in the Government's compelling small landowners who were opposed to hunting to transfer hunting rights over their land, on the basis of a law that presumed that hunting was an activity in which everyone wished to participate.

Where a government denies an individual access to her property over the course of many years, thereby preventing her from using it, enjoying it or exercising any control over its use, the right to peaceful enjoyment of possessions is violated. The Court arrived at this finding in the case of *Loizidou v. Turkey* (1996), in which it rejected a number of governmental arguments, including one that the political situation in Cyprus justified the continued denial of access. The Court observed that a "[H]indrance can amount to a violation of the Convention just like a legal impediment".

3. Control of the use of property

The Court has reviewed several cases in which owners of housing units have complained about governmental control over the use of the property. In addition to the *Mellacher* case mentioned above, which contested the imposition of rent controls, the Court has considered cases in which owners of flats were unable to have possession orders enforced against sitting tenants, arriving at different results in each. In the case of *Spadea and Scalabrino v. Italy* (1995), the Court found that the applicants had not established their need to live in the flats at issue, whereas the tenants were elderly women of modest means who had requested the city authorities to find them alternative low-income accommodation. There was thus no violation of Article 1 of Protocol No. 1. There was a violation in the case of *Scollo v. Italy* (1995), however, where the applicant had documented both his extensive physical disability and the need for him and his family to live in the flat at issue.

In a series of cases against Italy, the Court has consistently found violations of Article 1 of Protocol No. 1 where property owners have obtained final judicial decisions allowing them to regain possession of leased properties, but where the executive authorities have taken independent decisions about the scheduling of the evictions necessary to give force to those judgments, causing extensive delays (see, for example, *Immobiliare Saffi v. Italy* (1999)). It has also done so in other cases in which executive authorities have failed to comply with final judicial decisions (*Antonetto v. Italy* (2000) (failure to demolish an illegally constructed building), *Satka and Others v. Greece* (2003) (prolonged restrictions on the use of property as a result of successive decrees classifying the property for public use, depriving court decisions of their effect) and *Iatridis v. Greece* (1999) (refusal of executive authorities to return property to a tenant after the quashing of an eviction order)). A number of cases following this general pattern have arisen in States Parties that have undergone transitions to democracy and introduced various property restitution or compensation schemes with respect to properties that were nationalised under previous regimes. In some instances, the Court has found a "continuing violation" of Article 1 of Protocol No. 1 where an individual had obtained a valid judgment ordering the return of expropriated property, sometimes many years prior to the State's ratification of the Convention, but where the judgment had never been enforced (*Zwierzyński v. Poland* (2001) and *Vasilescu v. Romania* (1998)). (In these lines of cases, the Court often finds a violation of the right to a court under Article 6 of the Convention.)

Occasionally, the Court has reviewed cases complaining about the control of use of property in connection with criminal proceedings. In the case of *Raimondo v. Italy* (1994), the Italian authorities had sequestered a large amount of property belonging to a man suspected of mafia connections, pending proof that the property had been lawfully acquired. In finding no violation of Article 1 of Protocol 1, the Court stressed the uses to which the Mafia put properties such as the ones at issue, the difficulties faced by the Government in combating those uses, and the limited nature of the sequestration orders. The Court also found no violation in a case contesting the sequestration of a flat needed as evidence in connection with criminal proceedings (*Venditelli v. Italy* (1994)). In both these cases, the Court did find violations where the Government failed to take prompt action to re-establish full enjoyment of the use of the properties at the conclusion of the relevant proceedings.

4. Compensation for deprivations of property

The Court has reviewed many cases complaining about difficulties in obtaining compensation for deprivations of property. When considering whether particular governmental measures in this regard meet the standards required under Article 1 of Protocol No. 1, the Court will consider such factors as the complexity of the laws and procedures governing expropriation and compensation (*Zubani v. Italy* (1996)), the length of the proceedings relating to each of the two actions (*Zubani and Matos e Silva, Lda. and Others v. Portugal* (1996)), damage arising from the length of the deprivation (*Guillemin v. France* (1997)) and the adequacy of the amount of compensation in the light of delays in payment (*Guillemin and Akkuş v. Turkey* (1997)).

The Court has found violations of Article 1 of Protocol No. 1 where States Parties to the Convention have occasionally attempted through the operation of law to avoid meeting their obligations to compensate individuals for the expropriation of property (see, for example, *Former King of Greece and Others v. Greece* (2000)). A State may not unilaterally amend or terminate a contract with a private individual without paying compensation for the losses he or she has incurred, nor may a legislature act to nullify an award made in connection with such amendment or termination (*Stran Greek Refineries and Stratis Andreadis v. Greece* (1994)). Similarly, a government may not expunge by operation of law claims in tort against a particular group of individuals or the State, where those claims were previously perfected (*Pressos Compania Naviera S.A. and Others v. Belgium* (1995)).

It is worth noting that the inclusion of a reference to "general principles of international law" in Article 1 of Protocol No. 1 serves at least two purposes in connection with the obligation of the State to compensate individuals for property that the State has taken:

> Firstly, it enables non-nationals to resort directly to the machinery of the Convention to enforce their rights on the basis of the relevant principles of

international law, whereas otherwise they would have to seek recourse to diplomatic channels or to other available means of dispute settlement to do so. Secondly, the reference ensures that the position of non-nationals is safeguarded, in that it excludes any possible argument that the entry into force of Protocol No. 1 has led to a diminution of their rights (*James and Others v. the United Kingdom* (1986) and *Lithgow and Others v. the United Kingdom* (1986)).

The Court held that this difference in treatment does not constitute a violation of the prohibition of discrimination as laid down in Article 14 of the Convention, especially since there may well be good grounds for drawing a distinction between nationals and non-nationals as far as compensation is concerned, particularly regarding a taking of property effected in the context of a social reform. The Court emphasised that non-nationals are more vulnerable to domestic legislation since, unlike nationals, they will generally have played no part in the election or designation of its authors nor have been consulted on its adoption. Secondly, although the taking of property must always be effected in the public interest, different considerations may apply to nationals and non-nationals and there may well be a legitimate reason for requiring nationals to bear a greater burden in the public interest than non-nationals. However, the Court has also held that where a taking of property is unlawful, the principle of *restitutio in integrum* should apply equally to nationals and non-nationals (*Papamichalopoulos and Others v. Greece* (1993)).

5. Article 1 of Protocol No. 1 and other Articles of the Convention

Applicants often raise claims that not only has the State violated their right to property but that it has also failed to provide adequate procedural protections to contest the property issue, as required under Article 6 of the Convention. In the early cases raising these two claims, the Court often found that although the *substance* of States' actions under Article 1 of Protocol No. 1 may have fallen within the margin of appreciation, the quality of the *procedures* available to an individual wishing to challenge those actions often fell foul of the fair hearing requirements of Article 6(1) (*Allan Jacobsson* (1989); *Håkansson and Sturesson* (1990); *Langborger* (1989) all *v. Sweden*). The Court has more recently found violations of both Article 6 and Article 1 of Protocol No. 1 where the length of civil proceedings has had a disproportionately negative effect on the enjoyment of the right to property (*Luordo v. Italy* (2003)). Other contexts in which the Court has reviewed claims under both of these provisions are discussed in the preceding sections of this chapter.

Finally, as alluded to elsewhere, should a State fail to rebut allegations that it destroyed people's houses and movable property, the Court will find a violation of both the right to respect for the home under Article 8 and the right to property under Article 1 of Protocol No. 1 (*Akdivar and Others v. Turkey* (1996), *Selçuk and Asker v. Turkey* (1998) and several other cases against Turkey)). The Court found a "continuing violation" of these provisions in the inter-State case of *Cyprus v. Turkey* (2001) in two respects. First, it did so with regard to the denial to Greek Cypriot owners of property in northern Cyprus of access to and control, use and enjoyment of their property as well as any compensation for the interference with these property rights; and it also did so with regard to the failure of the authorities in northern Cyprus to secure the property rights of Greek Cypriots who departed from the territory or who wished to will their property to relatives living in the southern part of the island.

Chapter 14 – The right to education: Article 2 of Protocol No. 1

Protocol No. 1 – Article 2

> No person shall be denied the right to education. In the exercise of any functions which it assumes in relation to education and to teaching, the State shall respect the right of parents to ensure such education and teaching in conformity with their own religious and philosophical convictions.

There are three interrelated elements of the right to education under Article 2 of Protocol No. 1 to the Convention. In its first sentence, the Article provides that the State shall not deny anyone the right to education. This means that the State may not interfere with a person's exercise of the right to education, for instance by preventing him or her from availing himself or herself of the educational opportunities provided by the State. The second sentence of the Article sets forth two other elements of the right to education. First, it gives total discretion to the State to determine the nature and scope of its involvement with education and teaching. In general, this means that the State is under no obligation to provide certain kinds of educational opportunities or to guarantee that every individual receives the education he or she desires; and second, it guarantees the rights of parents to have their convictions respected in relation to their children's education.

In the case of *Kjeldsen, Busk Madsen and Pedersen v. Denmark* (1976), the Court emphasised the important role played by education in a democratic society, observing that the second sentence of Article 2 of Protocol No. 1 in particular:

> aims ... at safeguarding the possibility of pluralism in education, which possibility is essential for the preservation of the "democratic society" as conceived by the Convention.... in view of the power of the modern State, it is above all through State teaching that this aim must be realised.

Unlike many other Articles of the Convention guaranteeing the protection of substantive rights, Article 2 of Protocol No. 1 is framed in negative terms – that the State shall not deny rather than that the State shall guarantee respect for the right at issue. This construction of the right leaves the State in a good position to defend itself against charges of violations as an individual may find it difficult to pose a strong argument that a State has an obligation not to interfere and/or to act affirmatively to guarantee respect for the right to education. Instead, the individual has the burden of establishing that the State has actively denied the right to education – a much higher threshold than for the principles of non-interference or affirmative obligation. To the end of 2003, the Court has found the burden to be met in only two cases. In the inter-State case of *Cyprus v. Turkey* (2001), the applicant Government averred that the children of Greek Cypriots living in northern Cyprus were denied the right to education in that the Turkish Republic of Northern Cyprus (TRNC) had abolished secondary educational facilities that had previously met the linguistic and cultural needs of the children of Greek Cypriots. Before the Convention institutions, the respondent Government maintained that students wishing to obtain such an education were free to attend schools in the southern part of Cyprus. In finding a violation of Article 2 of Protocol No. 1, however, the Court noted that the respondent Government imposed restrictions on the return of Greek Cypriot children to the northern part of the island during and after the completion of their secondary education in the south, placing a disproportionate restriction on the enjoyment of family life as the burden to be borne for the exercise of the fundamental right to education. It also stressed that the respondent Government did, in fact, provide primary education in a Greek Cypriot environment and thus could be expected to continue to provide such education through the secondary school level as well.

In the case of *Campbell and Cosans v. the United Kingdom* (1982), the applicant mothers complained about the use of corporal punishment as a disciplinary measure in the State schools in Scotland attended by their children. The joined applications maintained, amongst other issues, that the use of corporal punishment in schools violated their rights under the second sentence of Article 2 of Protocol No. 1, to ensure that their children's education was in conformity with their philosophical convictions. The second applicant also contended that her son's suspension from school violated his right to education under the first sentence of the Article. The Court found a violation in both instances. It first addressed the United Kingdom Government's argument that functions relating to the internal administration of a school were not functions related to "education" and "teaching" within the meaning of Article 2, stating:

> The education of children is the whole process whereby, in any society, adults endeavour to transmit their beliefs, culture and other values to the young, whereas teaching or instruction refers in particular to the transmission of knowledge and to intellectual development....

> The use of corporal punishment may, in a sense, be said to belong to the internal administration of a school, but at the same time it is, when used, an integral part of the process whereby a school seeks to achieve the object for which it was established, including the development and moulding of the character and mental powers of its pupils.

The Court next examined the nature of the parents' philosophical convictions:

> Having regard to the Convention as a whole, the expression "philosophical convictions" in the present context denotes, in the Court's opinion, such convictions as are worthy of respect in a "democratic society"... and are not incompatible with human dignity; in addition, they must not conflict with the fundamental right of the child to education, the whole of Article 2 being dominated by its first sentence....

> The applicants' views relate to a weighty and substantial aspect of human life and behaviour, namely the integrity of the person, the propriety or otherwise of the infliction of corporal punishment and the exclusion of the distress which the risk

of such punishment entails. They are views which satisfy each of the various criteria listed above.

On finding a violation of the second sentence of Article 2 of Protocol No. 1, the Court then considered whether the State had violated the suspended child's right to education under the first sentence:

> [T]he existence of corporal punishment as a disciplinary measure in the school attended by her son ... underlay both ... allegations concerning Article 2, but there is a substantial difference between the factual basis of her two claims. In the case of the second sentence, the situation complained of was attendance at a school where recourse was had to a certain practice, whereas, in the case of the first sentence, it was the fact of being forbidden to attend; the consequences of the latter situation are more far-reaching than those of the former....
>
> Article 2 constitutes a whole that is dominated by its first sentence, the right set out in the second sentence being an adjunct of the fundamental right to education....
>
> Finally, there is also a substantial difference between the legal basis of the two claims, for one concerns a right of a parent and the other a right of a child....
>
> The right to education guaranteed by the first sentence of Article 2 by its very nature calls for regulation by the State, but such regulation must never injure with the substance of the right nor conflict with other rights enshrined in the Convention or its Protocols.

In addition to the case of *Cyprus v. Turkey* (2001), the Convention institutions have reviewed other complaints that a particular state policy or practice constitutes a de facto denial of the right to education. None of these complaints has been successful. In the case *"Relating to Certain Aspects of the Laws on the Use of Languages in Education in Belgium"* (*Belgian Linguistic* case) (1968)), the applicants, French-speaking residents living in the Dutch-speaking part of Belgium, complained that the Belgian Government's refusal to educate their children in French violated their rights under Article 2 of Protocol No. 1. The Court described the content and scope of the Article as follows:

> The negative formulation (of the right to education) indicates ... that the Contracting Parties do not recognise such a right to education as would require them to establish at their own expense, or to subsidise, education of any particular type or at any particular level....
>
> All member States of the Council of Europe ... possess a general and official educational system. There [is not] therefore, any question of requiring each State to establish such a system, but merely of guaranteeing to persons subject to the jurisdiction of the Contracting Parties the right, in principle, to avail themselves of the means of instruction existing at a given time....
>
> The first sentence of Article 2 of the Protocol consequently guarantees, in the first place, a right of access to educational institutions existing at a given time, but such access constitutes only a part of the right to education. For the "right to education" to be effective, it is further necessary that, *inter alia,* the individual who is the beneficiary should have the possibility of drawing profit from the education received, that is to say, the right to obtain , in conformity with the rules in

force in each State, and in one form or another, official recognition of the studies which he has completed....

The right to education guaranteed by the first sentence of Article 2 of the Protocol by its very nature calls for regulation by the State.... Such regulation must never injure the substance of the right to education nor conflict with other rights enshrined in the Convention.

Of the several issues raised by the applicants, the Court found a violation in only one instance. The Belgian legislation permitted Dutch-speaking children resident in certain French-speaking areas to have access to Dutch-language schools in other nearby regions, but did not accord the parallel right to French-speaking children. The Court held that this constituted a violation of the discrimination provision of Article 14 taken in conjunction with Article 2 of Protocol No. 1:

The residence condition is not imposed in the interest of schools, for administrative or financial reasons: it proceeds solely, in the case of the Applicants, from considerations relating to language. Furthermore the measure in issue does not fully respect, in the case of the majority of the Applicants and their children, the relationship of proportionality between the means employed and the aim sought....

The enjoyment of the right to education as the Court conceives it, and more precisely that of the right of access to existing schools, is not therefore on the point under consideration secured to everyone without discrimination on the ground, in particular, of language.

All of the above three cases dealt with access to education itself. The Convention institutions have also addressed more specifically the nature of respect for parental rights in the provision of education. The leading case on this matter is that of *Kjeldsen, Busk Madsen and Pedersen v. Denmark* (1976), in which several parents protested against the inclusion of sex education in Danish school curricula. The issue was complicated by the fact that, because the State integrated sex education into many subject areas, there was no means by which the State could easily respond to the parents' concerns, for example, by enabling them to withdraw their children from specific lessons offensive to their convictions. The Court described the philosophical basis of the "respect for parental rights" clause:

It is in the discharge of a natural duty towards their children – parents being primarily responsible for the "education and teaching" of their children – that parents may require the State to respect their religious and philosophical convictions. Their right thus corresponds to a responsibility closely linked to the enjoyment and the exercise of the right to education.

It then went on to describe the character of the State's responsibility in the area:

The second sentence of Article 2 implies on the other hand that the State, in fulfilling the functions assumed by it in regard to education and teaching, must take care that information or knowledge included in the curriculum is conveyed in an objective, critical and pluralistic manner. The State is forbidden to pursue an aim of indoctrination that might be considered as not respecting parents' religious and philosophical convictions. That is the limit that must not be exceeded.

The Court also held that the legality of private schools was not an adequate response to the parents' concerns, as it would lead to the unacceptable result that only the rights of wealthy parents would be "respected". Thus, although the State may allow students to withdraw from lectures that conflict with parental convictions, or to attend private schools, such options do not automatically relieve the State of its responsibilities to fulfil its obligations under Article 2 of Protocol No. 1 within the public school system. In this case, the Court held that although in principle sex education might involve the inculcation of value judgments, which practice could impinge upon parental rights, in this instance the Danish Government's actions were acceptable as their aim was to inform, not indoctrinate the students.

Chapter 15 – The right to free elections: Article 3 of Protocol No. 1

Protocol No. 1 – Article 3

> The High Contracting Parties undertake to hold free elections at reasonable intervals by secret ballot, under conditions which will ensure the free expression of the opinion of the people in the choice of the legislature.

Article 3 of Protocol No. 1 is the only substantive provision of the Convention that is not a right or a freedom, and that does not call for non-interference by the State. Instead, this provision clearly sets forth a positive obligation for the State. In the *Greek* case (1970), the Commission emphasised the importance of the rights guaranteed by Article 3 of Protocol No. 1, stating, "the existence of a representative legislature, elected at reasonable intervals, [is] the basis of a democratic society".

The Convention institutions have reviewed very few cases raising issues under Article 3 of Protocol 1. In the case of *Mathieu-Mohin and Clerfayt v. Belgium* (1987), the French-speaking applicants claimed that a Belgian legal requirement that candidates elected to the Flemish Council take their parliamentary oath in Dutch prevented French-speaking voters from voting for a French-speaking candidate, and thus violated the freedom of choice clause. At the outset, the Court emphasised that Article 3 of Protocol No. 1 is of "prime importance" in the Convention system, "since it enshrines a characteristic principle of democracy". The Court went on to hold that the Article did not require the establishment of any particular political system such as majority voting with one or two ballots or proportional representation. Nor did it require that all votes must be accorded equal weight in the tallying process or that all candidates must somehow be guaranteed equal chances of victory. The Court held that instead, the State's margin of appreciation, as exercised in light of the particular state of political evolution of the country concerned, leaves to the Commission and Court only the assessment of whether the conditions imposed by the State act to impair the essence of the protected rights.

In the case of *Gitonas and Others v. Greece* (1997) the Court found no violation of Article 3 of Protocol No. 1 where domestic law prohibited anyone who had held public office for more than three months in the three years prior to an election from standing as a candidate in that election. The Court came to the same conclusion in the case of *Ahmed and Others v. the United Kingdom* (1998), where the Government restricted the involvement of senior local government officers in certain types of political activity. In these cases, the Court considered that the protection of the right of others to effective political democracy constituted a legitimate aim and that placing temporary restrictions on some aspects of the political rights of civil servants, in the interests of securing their political impartiality, was not a disproportionate means to achieve that aim.

In the case of *Sadak and Others v. Turkey* (*No. 2*) (2002), the applicants had been forced to vacate their parliamentary seats following the dissolution of their political party by the Constitutional Court on the grounds that its former chairman had made certain speeches while abroad and that the party's central committee had issued a written declaration related to the situation of the Kurds in Turkey. The European Court of Human Rights found that the immediate and permanent dissolution of the political party in question and the resulting prohibition against the applicants' fulfilling their mandate constituted an extremely harsh measure that could not be regarded as proportionate to any legitimate aim relied on by the Government. The Court stressed that the measure "was incompatible with the very substance of the applicants' right to be elected and sit in parliament under Article 3 of Protocol 1 and infringed the sovereign power of the electorate who elected them as members of parliament."(paragraph 40)

The Court also found a violation of Article 3 of Protocol No. 1 where an applicant complained that her name had been removed from the list of candidates at a general election on the grounds that her knowledge of the sole working language in parliament did not meet the standard required under the domestic law. The Court accepted that the State could establish a single working language for its parliament and thus could impose language requirements on members of parliament. However, in the instant case, the Court found that the applicant had been held to a different standard than other electoral candidates and had been evaluated through means not provided for under the relevant law, full responsibility for assessing the applicant's linguistic knowledge being left to a single civil servant who had questioned the applicant about her political views, rather than testing her language skills (*Podkolzina v. Latvia* (2002)).

The Government suspended the voting rights of the applicant in *Labita v. Italy* (2000), on the grounds that he was suspected of being a member of the Mafia. Although the European Court of Human Rights considered that the temporary suspension of voting rights of persons against whom there is evidence of Mafia membership pursues a legitimate aim, it observed that these rights remained suspended once the applicant had been acquitted of relevant charges. It followed that the continued disenfranchisement of the applicant was not based on any concrete evidence on which a "suspicion" that the applicant belonged to the Mafia could be based. There had therefore been a violation of Article 3 of Protocol No. 1.

In the case of *Matthews v. the United Kingdom* (1999), the Court found a violation of Article 3 of Protocol No. 1 where a resident of Gibraltar attempted to register as a voter at the elections to the European Parliament, but was not permitted to do so on the grounds that an Act of the European Union limited the franchise for European Parliamentary elections to the United Kingdom only. In finding a violation, the Court noted that the European Parliament constituted an important legislative body of the European Union whose legislation affected the population of Gibraltar to the same extent as any other legislation in the domestic legal order. It also noted that the United Kingdom had extended the application of the European Convention on

Human Rights and Protocol No. 1 to Gibraltar well before the Act of the European Union at issue. Of particular interest in this case is the extensive discussion of the nature of a legislature in the sense of the Convention and the role of legislative authorities in effective political democracies.

Chapter 16 – Certain rights of nationals and aliens: Article 16, Articles 3 to 4 of Protocol No. 4, and Article 1 of Protocol No. 7

Protocol No. 4 – Article 3

1. No one shall be expelled, by means either of an individual or of a collective measure, from the territory of the State of which he is a national.

2. No one shall be deprived of the right to enter the territory of the State of which he is a national.

Protocol No. 4 – Article 4

Collective expulsion of aliens is prohibited.

Protocol No. 7 – Article 1

1. An alien lawfully resident in the territory of a State shall not be expelled therefrom except in pursuance of a decision reached in accordance with law and shall be allowed:

a. to submit reasons against his expulsion,

b. to have his case reviewed, and

c. to be represented for these purposes before the competent authority or a person or persons designated by that authority.

2. An alien may be expelled before the exercise of his rights under paragraph 1.a, b and c of this Article, when such expulsion is necessary in the interests of public order or is grounded on reasons of national security.

The Protocols to the Convention set forth several provisions relating to the rights of aliens, or aliens "lawfully resident" in the territory of the High Contracting Parties. The Convention itself sets forth only a provision restricting those rights, in its Article 16, which states:

Nothing in Articles 10, 11 and 14 shall be regarded as preventing the High Contracting Parties from imposing restrictions on the political activity of aliens.

This Article sets forth an exception to both the principle of non-discrimination under Article 14 and the principle that any High Contracting Party must secure to everyone within its jurisdiction the substantive rights and freedoms under the Convention. To date, the Court has reviewed only one case raising an issue under Article 16. In the case of *Piermont v. France* (1995), a German national who was a member of the European Parliament complained of certain restrictions on her freedom of expression and movement imposed upon her by the French authorities during a trip to French Polynesia. The French Government invoked Article 16 to justify the restrictions on her freedom of expression, an argument the court rejected on the grounds that she was not only a national of a member State of the European Union but a member of the European Parliament as well.

Article 3 of Protocol No. 4 prohibits a State from expelling its own nationals on either an individual or a collective basis. It also prohibits a State from depriving a national of the right to enter his or her own State. To date, the Court has not issued any judgments related to this provision.

Article 4 of Protocol No. 4 prohibits the collective expulsion of aliens. The Court clarified the scope of this provision in the case of *Čonka v. Belgium* (2002):

> [C]ollective expulsion, within the meaning of Article 4 of Protocol No. 4, is to be understood as any measure compelling aliens, as a group, to leave a country, except where such a measure is taken on the basis of a reasonable and objective examination of the particular case of each individual alien of the group.... (paragraph 59)

In this case, the Belgian authorities had summoned the applicant and his family to a police station, ostensibly for the purpose of filling out papers related to their pending requests for asylum. On their responding to the summons, they were arrested and deported together with a number of other individuals in similar circumstances. In light of prior pronouncements by political authorities that such operations would occur, instructions issued to the competent authorities for their implementation, the identical terms of the relevant arrest orders and similar factors, the Court found that there appeared to have been a collective expulsion. Taken in conjunction with the short time frame during which the deportations were effected, the difficulties the applicants faced in contacting a lawyer, and the fact that the asylum procedures had not been completed at the time, the Court found a lack of guarantees demonstrating that the individual circumstances of the applicants had been genuinely taken into account. There was thus a violation of Article 4 of Protocol No. 4.

The examination of cases of individual aliens is the focus of Article 1 of Protocol No. 7. The first paragraph of this Article prohibits the expulsion of any alien "lawfully resident" who has not been allowed to submit reasons against his or her expulsion, to have his or her case reviewed, and to be represented for these purposes before the authorities. The second paragraph, however, permits the State to expel an alien before his or her exercise of the listed rights "when such expulsion is necessary in the interests of public order or is grounded on reasons of national security". As of the end of 2003, the Court had not issued any judgments under Article 1 of Protocol No. 7.

Chapter 17 – The prohibition against discrimination: Article 14

Article 14

> The enjoyment of the rights and freedoms set forth in this Convention shall be secured without discrimination on any ground such as sex, race, colour, language, religion, political or other opinion, national or social origin, association with a national minority, property, birth or other status.

Unlike under other international human rights instruments, there is no general duty of non-discrimination in the Convention. Instead, the protection of Article 14 is accessory to the other substantive rights in the Convention: it has no independent life of its own. That being said, however, the Convention organs have stated that even if a State is found to have complied with its obligations to respect one of the substantive rights at issue in a given case, it may nevertheless be found to have violated that same right in conjunction with Article 14. For example, in the *Belgian Linguistic* case (1968), the Court found that although the right to education provided for under Article 2 of Protocol No. 1 was secured to all children in Belgium, the refusal to allow French-speaking students access to French language schools in the Brussels periphery due exclusively to the residence of the parents, whereas students from the Flemish-speaking community were not so limited, constituted prohibited discrimination.

1. Discrimination on the basis of sex

The European Court of Human Rights has reviewed a number of cases in which applicants have claimed that they have been discriminated against on the basis of their sex, with far fewer cases being brought by women than by men.

Discrimination against women

In the case of *Abdulaziz, Cabales, and Balkandali v. the United Kingdom* (1985), the three applicants claimed violations of Article 8 (family life) and Article 14 in the operation of United Kingdom immigration laws which made it more difficult for foreign men to join their fiancées or wives legally resident in the country than for foreign women to join their husbands. In finding no violation of Article 8, the Court noted that Contracting States have no obligation to respect a married couple's choice of country of residence and thereby to accept non-national spouses for settlement. However, the Court held that the United Kingdom had violated Article 14 in conjunction with Article 8, stating:

> The notion of discrimination within the meaning of Article 14 includes in general cases where a person or group is treated, without proper justification, less

favourably than another, even though the more favourable treatment is not called for by the Convention. (paragraph 82)

It is thus the inequity of particular treatment that is at issue under Article 14, not the comparison of different options a State chooses among when restricting the exercise of a given substantive right.

In the case of *Schuler-Zgraggen v. Switzerland* (1993), the authorities cancelled the disability pension of a woman who had given birth to a child, justifying their action by the assumption that she would have terminated her formal employment in order to become a full-time housewife and mother. In dismissing her appeal, an appeal court took as the sole basis for its reasoning the assumption that women give up work after childbirth. The Court found that there had been a difference of treatment based on sex and a violation of Article 6(1) (right to a fair trial) and Article 14, on the grounds that that difference had no reasonable or objective justification.

The Court found a violation of Article 1 of Protocol No. 1 and Article 14 in the case of *Wessels-Bergervoet v. the Netherlands* (2002). In this case, the applicant, a Dutch national, and her husband had always lived in the Netherlands. Her husband was granted a married person's old age pension at the legally mandated time, but at a reduced level as he had worked for a number of years in Germany and thus had not paid full contributions to the Dutch pension scheme. On meeting the requirements for retirement, the applicant was granted a pension that was reduced by the same amount as her husband's pension, ascribing his reduced rights also to her. Under the applicable law at the material time, a married man in the same situation would not have had his pension reduced.

Discrimination against men

The majority of cases in which men have complained of discrimination on the basis of sex have arisen in connection with the right to family life under Article 8. In the early case of *Rasmussen v. Denmark* (1984), a man wished to contest the paternity of a child borne by his wife, but was refused permission as the time limit to do so had run out. The wife, on the other hand, could apply for a paternity test at any time prior to the child's reaching the age of majority, should she have chosen to do so. The Court found no violation of Article 14 in conjunction with Article 8 (family life), as the Danish Government could justify a distinction between the situation of mothers and fathers.

The Court has reviewed several cases involving the rights of natural fathers to have access to their children, both under Article 8 with respect to violations of the right to family life and under Article 8 taken in conjunction with Article 14 with respect to allegations of discriminatory treatment as compared to that of divorced fathers. The participation of natural fathers in decisions relating to their children is normally the key element taken into consideration by the Court. For example, it found a violation of the right to family life and the prohibition against discrimination in the case of *Keegan v. Ireland* (1994) where the acknowledged father of a child born out of wedlock was neither consulted nor informed prior to the child being adopted. In the case of *Elsholz v. Germany* (2000), the Court found a violation of Article 8, but not of Article 14, given the substantive and in-depth review of the natural father's circumstances, which could not be considered to be less favourable than the review that would have been accorded to a divorced father. However, in several slightly later cases against Germany, the Court found that the laws governing access of natural fathers to their children did not provide adequate protection of the right to family life of natural fathers. The applicants' rights under Article 8, taken in conjunction with Article 14, had therefore been violated. (See, for example, *Hoffmann v. Germany* (2001) (violation of Articles 8 and 14, but not Article 8 alone), *Sommerfield v. Germany* (2003) and *Sahin v. Germany* (2003)). (In the latter two cases the Court found violations of Article 8 taken on its own as well.)

In *Karlheinz Schmidt v. Germany* (1994), the Court found a violation of Article 4 (prohibiting forced labour) taken in conjunction with Article 14 in the requirement that men serve in a public fire brigade or pay a fee to be released from the obligation. No such duty was placed on women.

In the case of *Van Raalte v. the Netherlands* (1997), the Court found a violation of Article 1 of Protocol No. 1 in conjunction with Article 14 where childless women over the age of forty-five were exempted from paying into a social fund for the benefit of children, whilst men of the same age were not; and in the case of *Willis v. the United Kingdom* (2002), the Court found a violation of the same provisions of the Convention where a widower was denied the same benefits as a widow, although his wife had for the greater part of their married life been the primary breadwinner and had paid full social security contributions as an employee until she had been forced to stop work due to illness.

The Court found a violation of Article 8 in connection with Article 14 on the grounds of discrimination on the basis of sex in the case of *Burghartz v. Switzerland* (1994) in which a man, upon marrying, was not permitted to put his name before his wife's and to take her name as the family name, whereas the opposite practice was permitted.

2. Discrimination on the basis of religion or belief

The Court has reviewed relatively few cases alleging violations of the right to freedom of religion or belief in conjunction with Article 14. To the end of 2003, the Court had found only one violation of Article 9 taken in conjunction with Article 14, in the case of *Thlimmenos v. Greece* (2000). In this case a Jehovah's Witness had been convicted of a felony for refusing to wear a military uniform. He was later refused admittance into the profession of chartered accountancy on the grounds that he was a convicted felon. The Court considered that although a State may have a legitimate interest in excluding some offenders from the profession, a conviction for refusing on religious or philosophical grounds to wear a military uniform could not be considered to imply any dishonesty or moral turpitude that would render someone unfit to enter the profession. It followed that there was no objective or reasonable justification for not treating the applicant differently from others convicted of a felony.

The right to family life was at issue in the case of *Hoffmann v. Austria* (1993). The applicant in this case was a woman who became a Jehovah's Witness, having previously been a Roman Catholic. At a later date, when she and her husband divorced, the Austrian courts awarded custody of their children to the husband, citing her religious affiliation as the sole grounds for the decision. The Court found a violation of her right to family life under Article 8 in conjunction with Article 14.

In the case of *Chassagnou and Others v. France* (1999), in which small rural landowners were required to join a hunters' association and to assign hunting rights to that association, but large landowners were not so compelled, the Court found a violation both of freedom of association guaranteed under Article 11 and Article 14 and of the right to property guaranteed under Article 1 of Protocol No. 1 and Article 14. The applicants in this case had declared their strong opposition to allowing hunting to take place on their land.

The Court found a violation of Article 6(1) and Article 14 in the case of *Canea Catholic Church v. Greece* (1997), in which it held that the refusal of the civil court to recognise the legal personality of the applicant church, whereas it did so for other religious denominations, constituted a violation both of the right of access to court and of the right not to be discriminated against in the enjoyment of that right.

3. Discrimination on the basis of citizenship or residency

The Court has found violations of the right to property guaranteed under Article 1 of Protocol No. 1 in conjunction with Article 14 in several cases in which citizenship of or permanent residency in a member State was the pivotal fact. In the case of *Darby v. Sweden* (1990), the applicant complained about the operation of a Swedish law requiring non-resident workers to pay a church tax from which resident workers could choose to be exempted. The Court held that such a restriction violated Protocol No. 1, Article 1 in conjunction with Article 14. The Court also found a violation of these provisions where the Austrian Government denied social benefits to a lawfully resident alien on the grounds that he was not a citizen, although he had made contributions to the national social fund (*Gaygusuz v. Austria* (1996)) and where the French Government refused to grant a disability allowance to a non-national who had been adopted as an adult by a French national (*Koua Poirrez v. France* (2003)).

The applicants in the cases of *Streletz, Kessler and Krenz v. Germany* (2001) and *K.-H.W. v. Germany* (2001) had been convicted of killing persons who had attempted to escape from the GDR into the FRG. In their complaint to the European Court of Human Rights, they alleged that, as former citizens of the GDR, they were disadvantaged in comparison with citizens of the FRG with respect to the protection afforded by the constitutional principle of the non-retroactive application of criminal law, guaranteed also under Article 7 of the European Convention on Human Rights. However, the Court considered that the principles applied by the German Federal Constitutional Court were equally valid in respect of persons who were not former nationals of the GDR. It thus found no discrimination contrary to Article 14 of the Convention taken together with Article 7.

In the case of *Magee v. the United Kingdom* (2000), the Court found that any difference in treatment of individuals arrested and detained in Northern Ireland and those arrested and detained in other parts of the United Kingdom could be explained in terms of geographical location and did not stem from the personal characteristics to which Article 14 referred.

4. Discrimination on the basis of birth

In several early cases complaining of discrimination against children born out of wedlock the Court established the important principle that any differential treatment by the State of individuals in similar situations must have an objective and reasonable justification. The Court held that this standard was not met in the case of *Marckx v. Belgium* (1979), in which a mother and her natural child claimed violations of Protocol No. 1, Article 1 (property), Article 8 (family life) and Article 14 in the operation of the Belgian legal regime applicable to children born out of wedlock. The Court held that the situations of both mother and child were sufficiently analogous to those between a married woman and her child that the State could not justify the differential treatment it had imposed. The sole exception was in relation to the child's claims that her right to property under Protocol No. 1, Article 1 was violated: the Court held this provision inapplicable to an expectation of inheritance. When a new pair of applicants in the same circumstances as in the *Marckx* case filed an application twelve years later, the Court reaffirmed its holding (*Vermeire v. Belgium* (1991)).

The Court applied the same principles in the case of *Inze v. Austria* (1987), finding a violation in the application of an Austrian inheritance law that gave precedence to children born in wedlock over those born out of wedlock when attributing agricultural land on the intestacy of the parent. There have been a number of cases raising similar issues since *Inze* was decided. In the case of *Mazurek v. France* (2000) for example, the applicant was the child of an adulterous union. Under the applicable law, his rights to inherit from his mother were limited to half of what his entitlement would have been had he been legitimate; there had thus been a violation of Article 1 of Protocol No. 1 taken together with Article 14 of the Convention. In the case of *Camp and Bourimi v. the Netherlands* (2000), the Court found a violation of Article 8 taken in conjunction with Article 14, where a child whose natural father died before the child was born and who was declared legitimate – but without retroactive effect – two years after his birth, was excluded from inheriting from his father as he had been born out of wedlock and had not been legally recognised by his father.

5. Discrimination on the basis of "other status"

Discrimination based on sexual orientation

Given the date of the drafting of the Convention, it is no surprise that the anti-discrimination provisions do not specifically list "sexual orientation" as a ground of prohibited discrimination. However, the catch-all phrase "other status" has been invoked successfully in this regard, at least in recent years, the Court noting that "[j]ust like differences based on sex, differences based on sexual orientation require particularly serious reasons by way of justification" (*Smith and Grady v. the United Kingdom* (2000)). The Court found a violation of the right to private life guaranteed under Article 8 in conjunction with Article 14 with respect to ages of consent for homosexual acts between adults and adolescents that were different from those for heterosexual or lesbian relations (*L. and V. v. Austria* (2003) and *S.L. v. Austria* (2003). In addition to finding that homosexuals have the right to private life, the Court has also established the principle that homosexuals have a right to family life, including with any children they might have. In the case of *Salgueiro da Silva Mouta v. Portugal* (1999), the Court found a violation of Article 8 taken together with Article 14 where parental rights granted to a father on divorce were later overturned in favour of the mother, on the ground that the applicant was a homosexual and living with another man. However, the Court did not find a violation of these two provisions in a case in which a homosexual man complained that the government had unlawfully discriminated against him when it dismissed his request for authorisation to adopt a child, implicitly on the grounds of his homosexuality. The Court noted both that the Convention did not guarantee, as such, the right to adopt children, and that there was very little common ground between the member States of the Council of Europe with respect to the issue (*Fretté v. France* (2002)).

The Court also found a violation of the right to respect for the home in conjunction with the prohibition against discrimination where the surviving partner of a homosexual relationship was not permitted to continue to occupy a rented apartment on the death of his partner, whereas others in stable relationships could do so (*Karner v. Austria* (2003)).

Other grounds invoked as discriminatory

The applicant in the case of *Bucheň v. the Czech Republic* (2002), a military judge at the time the Czech Constitution abolished military courts, was dismissed from the armed forces, which dismissal in principle entitled him to receive a military pension. At the time of the transition, he agreed to be transferred to a judicial position in a civilian court. Subsequently, he was denied his military pension on the basis of a law that suspended the payment of such pensions to former military judges who had agreed to be transferred to the ordinary courts until the end of their terms of office as judges. The Court found a violation of the right to property and the prohibition against discrimination, noting that at least two categories of former members of the regular armed forces continued to receive a pension and that the government could not justify the differential treatment of the applicant.

In the case of *Van der Mussele v. Belgium* (1983), a Belgian trainee lawyer required to undertake a certain number of uncompensated cases for indigent clients complained of a violation of Articles 4 (forced labour) and 14. The Court held that the State was justified in imposing such a requirement on lawyers, as not only were lawyers in a different position from other professionals who were not under the same obligation (dentists, doctors, judges and others), but also the contested practice was one means by which Belgium could implement another right guaranteed by the Convention (fair trial under Article 6).

In general, the Court permits States a wide margin of appreciation with respect to the regulation of residential rental property, and is disinclined to find discrimination in regard to claims made by landlords over tenants who may be entitled to live at low cost in rental properties through the operation of legal or regulatory regimes established to resolve severe housing problems for indigent or disabled people. For example, the Court found no violation of Protocol No. 1, Article 1 in conjunction with Article 14 where the Italian Government placed restrictions on the right of certain landlords to regain property they had rented out. However, the Court also held that the State could legitimately draw distinctions between residential and non-residential property in this regard (*Spadea and Scalabrino v. Italy* (1995) and *Edoardo Palumbo v. Italy* (2000)). Where an individual has rented a home from the State under a contract that in all material aspects is comparable to a normal rental contract between private parties, the Court has held that the State cannot treat that individual differently from tenants renting property from private individuals (*Larkos v. Cyprus* (1999) (violation of the right to respect for the home under Article 8 in conjunction with Article 14)).

The applicants in the case of *Pine Valley Developments and Others v. Ireland* (1991) had purchased land on the strength of an outline planning permission that was later nullified by the Supreme Court. A law was subsequently enacted that validated all permissions affected by the Supreme Court decision except those of the applicants. The European Court of Human Rights found that the different treatment of the applicants constituted prohibited discrimination in conjunction with the right to property guaranteed under Article 1 of Protocol No. 1 to the Convention.

6. A few words about Protocol No. 12

As noted at the beginning of this chapter, the prohibition against discrimination guaranteed under Article 14 is of relatively narrow applicability. In 2000, the Council of Europe opened for signature and ratification Protocol No. 12 to the Convention, which states in part:

> Reaffirming that the principle of non-discrimination does not prevent States Parties from taking measures in order to promote full and effective equality, provided that there is an objective and reasonable justification for those measures....

> 1. The enjoyment of any right set forth by law shall be secured without discrimination on any ground such as sex, race, colour, language, religion, political or

other opinion, national or social origin, association with a national minority, property, birth or other status.

Thus, Protocol No. 12 introduces the idea that States may take affirmative action to promote full and effective equality in appropriate circumstances, without falling foul of the prohibition against discrimination. It also extends the principle of non-discrimination to domestic law, rather than just to rights guaranteed by the Convention. As of the end of 2003, five countries had ratified this Protocol. Ten countries must ratify the Protocol for it to enter into force.

Chapter 18 – The right to an effective domestic remedy: Article 13

Article 13

> Everyone whose rights and freedoms as set forth in this Convention are violated shall have an effective remedy before a national authority notwithstanding that the violation has been committed by persons acting in an official capacity.

Article 13 of the Convention guarantees "an effective remedy before a national authority" to anyone whose rights and freedoms under the Convention have been violated. The right established by Article 13 flows as a logical consequence from Article 1, which imposes on the High Contracting Parties the obligation to "secure" the rights and freedoms under the Convention. The provision of domestic remedies to uphold these rights and freedoms can be seen as part of that obligation. In an important case delineating the scope of Article 13, the Court established that it both extends to any claim that can be considered to be "arguable" under the Convention and requires domestic authorities not only to decide such claim but to provide redress in the event that they find a violation (*Silver and Others v. the United Kingdom* (1983)). Although review by a judicial authority is not necessary, any other competent authority must have comparable powers and guarantees (*Silver and P.G. and J.H. v. the United Kingdom* (2001)).

1. "Arguable" claim under Article 13

Although the wording of Article 13 calls for an effective remedy for a "violation" of a Convention right or freedom, in the case of *Klass and Others v. Germany* (1978) the Court held that, whereas an individual might only be entitled to a domestic remedy in instances where a "violation" has occurred, this does not mean that the State can permanently disenfranchise an individual from establishing such a "violation" before a national authority by rendering it impossible to lodge an effective complaint with a competent national authority (see also *Metropolitan Church of Bessarabia and Others v. Moldova* (2001)). Consequently, a finding of a violation of the Convention cannot logically be a prerequisite for the application of Article 13. It follows that the Court itself may find a violation of Article 13 in a case in which it does not find a violation of any other provision of the Convention, as long as an applicant can show that he or she had an "arguable" claim under one or more of the other provisions (*Valsamis v. Greece* (1996), *Efstratiou v. Greece* (1996) and *Camenzind v. Switzerland* (1997)).

2. "Effectiveness" of remedies in the sense of Article 13

The protection afforded by Article 13 is not absolute, some limitations on the conceivable remedy being inherent in the context in which an alleged violation – or category of violations – has occurred. In such circumstances the Court does not treat Article 13 as being inapplicable but treats its requirement of an "effective remedy" as meaning "a remedy that is as effective as can be, having regard to the restricted scope for recourse inherent [in the particular context]" (*Klass and Others v. Germany* (1978)). In the *Klass* case, and a number of other similar cases, the context has been the tapping of telephone lines or the surveillance of the applicant in connection with a criminal investigation. In these cases, the Court has noted that such measures would be of little utility if the individual who was the subject of them was aware that they were taking place. It none the less has considered that "effectiveness" in this context requires such protections for the individual as notification that surveillance measures were applied to him or her at a reasonable point after the grounds necessitating the surveillance have ceased, recourse to an independent authority to contest the surveillance or its effects on protected rights, the possibility to bring a civil claim for any damage suffered as a result of the surveillance, and so forth. Also in this context, the Court has held that the exclusion at trial of evidence gained through any unlawful surveillance activity is necessary but not sufficient as a remedy for any violation of the right to private life that may have occurred (*Khan v. the United Kingdom* (2000) and *Taylor-Sabori v. the United Kingdom* (2002)).

In a series of cases in which the applicants were subjected to extradition or deportation on the basis of grounds asserted by executive authorities, the Court has held that "effectiveness" requires that a decision to this effect by an executive authority must be subject to independent review in an adversarial proceeding before a body with the capacity to review the factual basis for the grounds asserted by the executive, to balance the public interest asserted by the State with the individual right at issue and to reject the executive's assertion in this regard (see, for example, *Chahal v. the United Kingdom* (1996), *Jabari v. Turkey* (2000) and *Al-Nashif v. Bulgaria* (2002). With respect to expulsions from a State Party, the effectiveness of a remedy also presupposes that the remedy available can prevent the execution of measures contrary to the Convention, where the consequences of those measures would be irreversible (*Čonka v. Belgium* (2002) (violation of Article 13 and Article 4 of Protocol No. 4, prohibiting the collective expulsion of aliens)).

In a few cases, the Court has considered the "effectiveness" of a remedy in light of the impossibility of challenging the operation of a domestic law or regulation that, on its face, violates a protected right under the Convention. For example, in the case of *Abdulaziz, Cabales and Balkandali v. the United Kingdom* (1985), the three applicants, women with permanent resident status in the United Kingdom, challenged immigration regulations which permitted men with the same status to bring their spouses into the country but prohibited women from doing so. Because the regulations were explicit on this point and because no possibility existed to request that they be overridden in particular cases, the Court found a violation of the rights of the women to an effective domestic remedy under Article 13. Similarly, the Court found a violation of Article 13 where domestic prison rules themselves were contrary to the Convention, for example, with respect to restrictions placed on certain types of correspondence (see, for example, *Campbell and Fell v. the United Kingdom* (1984)). However, in most cases claiming violations of Article 13 with respect to control or censorship of the correspondence of persons in detention, the Court has found violations based on the delegation of the power to exercise discretion in this area to officials in charge of detention facilities, coupled with the failure to provide any recourse against arbitrary or unduly restrictive actions they may take in this regard.

Subject to compliance with the requirements of the Convention, Contracting States are afforded some discretion as to the manner in which they provide the relief required by Article 13 (*Kaya v. Turkey* (1998)). However, although the scope of the Contracting States' obligations under Article 13 varies depending on the nature of the applicant's complaint, the remedy required by Article 13 must be "effective" in practice as well as in law (*İlhan v. Turkey* (2000)). This requirement has led the Court to find that a claim based on the constitutional right to justice and to litigate does not constitute an effective domestic remedy for excessively long proceedings for the purposes of Article 13 of the Convention (*Doran v. Ireland* (2003)). The Court has interpreted the term "effective" to mean that the remedy must be adequate and accessible and that it must itself meet requirements of speediness (*Paulino Tomás v. Portugal* (2003)). Where an individual claims that available domestic remedies are ineffective, the Court has held that the respondent Government must show their effective application in one or more similar cases (*Vereinigung demokratischer Soldaten Österreichs and Gubi v. Austria* (1994), *Valsamis v. Greece* (1996) and *Efstratiou v. Greece* (1996)).

3. Relationship between Article 13 and other Articles of the Convention

In addition to Article 13, two other provisions of the Convention explicitly require States to provide remedies for violations of protected rights: Article 5(4) (habeas corpus) and Article 6(1) (fair hearing). Because these provisions both require access to the judiciary, for many years the Convention institutions considered that it was unnecessary to rule on a complaint under Article 13 of the Convention in cases also raising issues under one of these provisions. Although this is still the case with respect to Article 5(4), the proliferation of applications to the Court in which the only, or principal, allegation has been the failure of domestic authorities to ensure a hearing within a reasonable time, as guaranteed under Article 6(1) of the Convention, led the Court to revisit its long-standing position that a finding of a violation of that provision obviated the need to address any related claim framed in terms of Article 13 (see, for example, *Bouilly v. France* (1999)). In the case of *Kudla v. Poland* (2000), the Court finally held that the right to trial within a reasonable time is less effective if there exists no opportunity to submit the Convention claim first to a national authority; and thus that the requirements of Article 13 should be seen as reinforcing those of Article 6(1), instead of as being absorbed by the general obligation imposed by the latter provision, at least with respect to inordinate delays in legal proceedings. In the circumstances of the case, there was thus a violation of Article 13 due to the lack of any effective domestic remedy against undue delays in judicial proceedings. In this case, the Court also elaborated on the nature of effective remedies in this context, stressing that such remedies must be able to prevent the alleged violation or its continuation and/or to provide adequate redress for any violation that had already occurred.

Many individuals submitting applications to the Court have alleged that no effective remedy existed with respect to the failure of domestic authorities to provide redress for unlawful deaths or prohibited ill-treatment. The Court scrutinises such allegations particularly rigorously given that these rights rank as the most fundamental under the Convention. In such cases, the Court has considered that an effective investigation for the purposes of Article 13 comprises a thorough and effective investigation capable of leading to the effective identification and punishment of those responsible for an alleged violation of a Convention right, effective access of the complainant to the investigatory procedure and payment of compensation to the victim, where appropriate (*Aksoy v. Turkey* (1996), *Aydin v. Turkey* (1997), *Assenov and Others v. Bulgaria* (1998), *İlhan v. Turkey* (2000) and *Keenan v. the United Kingdom* (2001)). The same principles apply with respect to arguable claims of violation of the right to life guaranteed under Article 2 (*Tanli v. Turkey* (2001), *Tanrıkulu v. Turkey* (1999), *Velikova v. Bulgaria* (2000) and *Çiçek v. Turkey* (2001)). Should the only channel for launching an investigation into an alleged violation of a fundamental right be through the initiative of an executive authority, there will be a violation of Article 13 if that authority fails to act on being informed that such a violation may have occurred (*Egmez v. Cyprus* (2000)). The Court has considered that the failure to act of a governmental official with the duty to investigate may be tantamount to undermining the effectiveness of any other remedies that may have existed at the material time. In this respect it is important to note that the Court has found that an important aspect of an effective remedy is compensation that reflects the pain, stress, anxiety and frustration that transpire in circumstances giving rise to claims under these important Articles. Where no possibility exists to apply for compensation for non-pecuniary damages suffered by a victim of such a severe violation of rights, the Court will find a violation of Article 13 (*Paul and Audrey Edwards v. the United Kingdom* (2002) and *McGlinchey v. the United Kingdom* (2003)).

In addition to cases arising in connection with Articles 2 and 3 of the Convention, the Court has also applied the principles outlined above to cases raising claims that the governmental authorities had failed to respond adequately to allegations that security forces had destroyed people's homes (see, for example, *Mentes and Others v. Turkey* (1997) and several other similar cases).

Chapter 19 – Derogations in time of war or other public emergency: Article 15

Article 15

1.   In time of war or other public emergency threatening the life of the nation any High Contracting Party may take measures derogating from its obligations under this Convention to the extent strictly required by the exigencies of the situation, provided that such measures are not inconsistent with its other obligations under international law.

2.   No derogation from Article 2, except in respect of deaths resulting from lawful acts of war, or from Articles 3, 4 (paragraph 1) and 7 shall be made under this provision.

3.   Any High Contracting Party availing itself of this right of derogation shall keep the Secretary General of the Council of Europe fully informed of the measures which it has taken and the reasons therefor. It shall also inform the Secretary General of the Council of Europe when such measures have ceased to operate and the provisions of the Convention are again being fully executed.

There are several means by which a High Contracting Party to the Convention may limit the exercise of the rights guaranteed. At the time of ratification, a State may lodge a reservation relating to one of the substantive provisions of the Convention (see discussion on reservations below), and when responding to a petition claiming that it has violated one of the rights protected by the Convention, it may invoke any restrictive clauses applicable under such Articles as 8 to 11 (see discussion above). Article 15 of the Convention also permits States to restrict the exercise of many of the rights under the Convention, but it may do so only in certain well-defined and exceptional circumstances, and in accordance with specific procedures. Article 15 is not to be lightly invoked.

As is appropriate to such a serious matter as derogation from a human rights treaty, Article 15 prescribes a very strict standard for States that wish to derogate from the European Convention on Human Rights. In the case of *Lawless v. Ireland* (1961), a member of the Irish Republican Army claimed that the procedures and conditions of his detention by the Irish Government constituted a violation of Article 5 of the Convention. The European Court of Human Rights set forth the criteria for evaluating the existence of the conditions dictated by Article 15, according to "the natural and customary meaning of the words":

> The existence ... of a "public emergency threatening the life of the nation," [can be derived] from a combination of several factors, namely: in the first place, the existence in the territory of the Republic of Ireland of a secret army engaged in unconstitutional activities and using violence to attain its purposes; second, the fact that this army was also operating outside the territory of the State, thus seriously jeopardising the relations of the Republic of Ireland with its neighbour; thirdly, the steady and alarming increase in terrorist activities....

The Court assessed the Irish Government's specific measures of derogation in light of the "strictly required by the exigencies of the situation" criterion:

> In the judgment of the Court ... the application of the ordinary law had proved unable to check the growing danger which threatened the Republic of Ireland ... the ordinary criminal courts, or even the special criminal courts or military courts, could not suffice to restore peace and order ... the amassing of the necessary evidence to convict persons involved in activities of the IRA ... was meeting with great difficulties caused by the military, secret and terrorist character of those groups and the fear they created among the population ... the sealing of the border would have had extremely serious repercussions on the population as a whole, beyond the extent required by the exigencies of the emergency....

> Moreover, the Offences against the State (Amendment) Act of 1940, was subject to a number of safeguards designed to prevent abuses in the operation of the system of administrative detention ... the application of the Act was ... subject to constant supervision by Parliament, which not only received precise details of its enforcement at regular intervals but could also at any time, by a Resolution, annul the Government's Proclamation which had brought the Act into force....

> Immediately after the Proclamation which brought the power of detention into force, the Government publicly announced that it would release any person detained who gave an undertaking to respect the Constitution and the Law and not to engage in any illegal activity.... Persons arrested were informed immediately after their arrest that they would be released following the undertaking in question ... the existence of this guarantee of release given publicly by the Government constituted a legal obligation on the Government to release all persons who gave the undertaking.

The Court held that both the measures themselves and their application to Lawless could be characterised as measures strictly required by the exigencies of the situation within the meaning of Article 15 of the Convention.

In the *Greek* case (1969), the Commission clarified that the term "public emergency" contained the notion of imminent danger and that therefore the following elements were required to meet the standard established by Article 15:

1. It must be actual or imminent.

2. Its effects must involve the whole nation.

3. The continuance of the organised life of the community must be threatened.

4. The crisis or danger must be exceptional, in that the normal measures or restrictions, permitted by the Convention for the maintenance of public safety, health and order, are plainly inadequate.

The Commission then found that the Greek Government had not met its burden of proof in establishing the existence of these conditions.

In the case of *Ireland v. the United Kingdom* (1978), the Commission addressed explicitly the application of the principle of proportionality inherent in Article 15. It noted that a government may not invoke the existence of a state of emergency to justify any possible measure it might choose to implement, but it must establish a concrete connection between the measure and the situation requiring control. At the same time, the Commission found that a government must be allowed to improve particular measures without afterwards being found guilty of a violation of Article 15.

Since the Convention's entry into force, member States have registered derogations under Article 15. The United Kingdom, for example, has registered derogations, principally relating to Articles 5 and 6 of the Convention, for several of their colonies (prior to their independence from the United Kingdom) and for Northern Ireland. For example, the United Kingdom registered a derogation from Article 5 in relation to the operation of the Prevention of Terrorism Act, after the European Court of Human Rights had held that the United Kingdom Government violated Article 5 by detaining, without charge or appropriate procedural safeguards, persons suspected of participating in "terrorist" activities (*Brogan and Others v. the United Kingdom* (1988)).

Turkey registered its first derogation in 1961 in relation to its entire national territory. The Turkish Government subsequently revoked this derogation, but registered a new one applicable only to selected cities for certain specified periods. Since that time, Turkey has registered derogations for these or other cities on a number of occasions. The Court has held that a government may not extend a derogation with a limited geographic scope to cover areas not included within its remit (*Sakik and Others v. Turkey* (1997)).

Greece registered its first derogation after the April 1967 coup d'état and several others between that date and 1969 when the Greek Government denounced the Convention. Greece withdrew from the Council of Europe shortly thereafter, but later rejoined the organisation. It became a party to the Convention again in 1974.

The Republic of Ireland has twice exercised its powers of derogation in connection with the implementation of its Emergency Powers Act.

Article 15(2) prohibits derogations from Articles 2, 3, 4 and 7 of the Convention. This prohibition is absolute as regards Article 3 (torture, inhuman and degrading treatment or punishment) and Article 4(1) (slavery). Slavery is the only non-derogable right under Article 4 because it relates to the total status or situation of the person, whereas the other rights guaranteed by the Article relate to work of an involuntary but incidental or temporary character.

The prohibition against derogations in respect of the right to life is weaker than the other prohibitions. Article 15(2) itself permits a State to derogate from Article 2 of the Convention "in respect of deaths resulting from lawful acts of war". The sixth Protocol, concerning the Abolition of the Death Penalty, prohibits derogations from its provisions and yet its Article 2 allows States to provide for the death penalty "in respect of acts committed in time of war or of imminent threat of war", a broader category of exceptions than is set forth in Article 15(2) of the Convention itself.

Chapter 20 – Reservations and interpretative declarations

Under the Convention, a State may limit the operation and effect of Articles protecting specific substantive rights by lodging "reservations" to the relevant Article or Articles. According to Article 2(1)(d) of the United Nations Convention on the Law of Treaties of 1969, which has, in many respects, codified general principles of treaty interpretation, a reservation is:

> a unilateral statement, however phrased or named, made by a State, when signing, ratifying, accepting, approving or acceding to a treaty, whereby it purports to exclude or to modify the legal effect of certain provisions of the treaty in their application to that State....

Because the operation of the European Convention on Human Rights is not based on the principle of reciprocity between States, but instead on the High Contracting Parties' acceptance of unilateral obligations, the Vienna Convention provides little guidance as to the effect of States' reservations to the Convention.

Article 57 of the European Convention on Human Rights reads:

> 1.   Any State may, when signing this Convention or when depositing its instrument of ratification, make a reservation in respect of any particular provision of the Convention to the extent that any law then in force in its territory is not in conformity with the provision. Reservations of a general character shall not be permitted under this Article.

> 2.   Any reservation made under this Article shall contain a brief statement of the law concerned.

The Article thus lays down three conditions for the admissibility of reservations: (a) the reservation must be the direct consequence of a national law that is not in conformity with a provision of the Convention (it being understood that the law must be in force when the reservation is made); (b) the reservation must be made in respect of a particular provision of the Convention; and (c) the reservation must indicate which provisions of domestic law are affected. To date, the Convention institutions have not distinguished between the terms "reservation" and "interpretative declaration", the latter term referring to a given country's statement that its acceptance to be bound by a given treaty provision is conditioned on a particular interpretation of that provision. Both reservations and interpretative declarations restrict the effect and operation of a given treaty provision on the State involved.

The first condition of Article 57 prohibits a State from lodging a reservation in relation to any law passed after it has ratified the Convention: the second permits a State to lodge a reservation only in respect of a "particular provision" of the Convention. In spite of the literal wording of Article 57, the Commission has permitted States to adopt new laws or regulations that are the same in substance as those in force at the time when the original reservation was lodged. The Court considers that it does not have to review the validity of a reservation with respect to a law promulgated after ratification of the Convention, given that reservations must refer to specific domestic laws in force at the time the reservation is lodged. It follows that it also will review the substance of a claim with respect to which a State invokes such a reservation (*Fischer v. Austria* (1995)).

The Court has held that a State may not make a reservation in relation to an Article of the Convention that does not deal directly with substantive rights and freedoms, but instead with procedural or formal matters. In the case of *Loizidou v. Turkey* (1995), the applicant challenged the attempt by the Turkish Government to impose restrictions on the exercise of the right of individual petition and the jurisdiction of the Court, at a time when the acceptance of these two mechanisms was optional. In finding such restrictions impermissible, the Court stated:

> If ... substantive or territorial restrictions were permissible under these provisions, Contracting Parties would be free to subscribe to separate regimes of enforcement of Convention obligations.... Such a system ... would not only seriously weaken the role of the ... Court ... but would also diminish the effectiveness of the Convention as a constitutional instrument of European public order (*ordre public*).

The last sentence of paragraph 1 of Article 57 prohibits reservations "of a general character". In the case of *Belilos v. Switzerland* (1988), the applicant complained that the impossibility of appeal to a court against a decision taken by an administrative authority constituted a violation of the right to fair trial under Article 6(1) of the Convention. In responding to her complaint, the Swiss Government referred to its interpretative declaration on Article 6(1), which reads:

> The Swiss Federal Council considers that the guarantee of fair trial in Article 6, paragraph 1 of the Convention, in the determination of civil rights and obligations or any criminal charge against the person in question is intended solely to ensure ultimate control by the judiciary over the acts or decisions of the public authorities relating to such rights or obligations or the determination of such a charge.

The Convention institutions found that the wording of the declaration had the effect of almost entirely depriving a criminal defendant of the protection of the Convention, and hence the declaration had too general a scope to be compatible with the requirements of Article 57, at least as regards criminal proceedings. The Court explained:

> By "reservation of a general character" in Article [57] is meant in particular a reservation couched in terms that are too vague or broad for it to be possible to determine their exact meaning and scope ... the words "ultimate control by the judiciary over the acts or decisions of the public authorities"... do not make it possible for the scope of the undertaking by Switzerland to be ascertained exactly, in particular as to which categories of dispute are included and as to whether or not the "ultimate control by the judiciary" takes in the facts of the case. They can therefore be interpreted in different ways, whereas Article [57], paragraph 1, requires

precision and clarity. In short, they fall foul of the rule that reservations must not be of a general character.

Following the judgment in the *Belilos* case, the Swiss Government annulled the reservation with regard to criminal charges and to proceedings concerning the determination of a civil right or obligation under Article 6.

Paragraph 2 of Article 57 provides that "[a]ny reservation under this Article shall contain a brief statement of the law concerned." This provision essentially supplements the requirements of paragraph 1 that a reservation relate to a law "then in force" and that it not be of a general character. The purpose of paragraph 2 is to ensure that States lodging a reservation to the Convention provide sufficient information to enable the Commission and Court to assess its legitimacy. In the case of *Weber v. Switzerland* (1990), the applicant claimed a violation of his right to a public hearing in the determination of a criminal charge against him. The Swiss Government responded by referring to the following reservation:

> The rule contained in Article 6, paragraph 1, of the Convention that hearings shall be in public shall not apply to proceedings relating to the determination ... of any criminal charge which, in accordance with cantonal legislation, are heard before an administrative authority.

> The rule that judgment must be pronounced publicly shall not affect the operation of cantonal legislation on civil or criminal procedure providing that judgment shall not be delivered in public but notified to the parties in writing.

The Court held this reservation to be invalid on the grounds that the Swiss Government failed to append "a brief statement of the law [or laws] concerned", as required by Article 57(2). Referring to the above-mentioned Belilos case, the Court emphasised that this omission constituted a breach of a condition of substance, not just a formal requirement. The Court arrived at a similar finding in the case of *Eisenstecken v. Austria* (2000), with respect to a reservation stating that:

> The provisions of Article 6 of the Convention shall be so applied that there shall be no prejudice to the principles governing public court hearings laid down in Article 90 of the 1929 version of the Federal Constitution Law.

The Court noted that that the reservation in issue did not contain a "brief statement" of the law which was considered as not conforming to Article 6 of the Convention. The Court stated:

> From the wording of the reservation it might be inferred that Austria intended to exclude from the scope of Article 6 all proceedings in civil and criminal matters before ordinary courts – and even all kinds of other quasi-judicial bodies – in so far as particular laws allowed for non-public hearings. However, a reservation which merely refers to a permissive, non-exhaustive, provision of the Constitution and which does not refer to, or mention, those specific provisions of the Austrian legal order which exclude public hearings, does not "afford to a sufficient degree 'a guarantee ... that [it] does not go beyond the provision expressly excluded' by Austria".

Chapter 21 – Procedures under the European Convention on Human Rights

Article 19 of the European Convention on Human Rights states that the primary task of the European Court of Human Rights is to "ensure the observance of the engagements" undertaken by the High Contracting Parties to the Convention. The Court cannot act on its own to examine the human rights situation in a particular country. The initiative to set the international control mechanism in motion lies with individuals or with the High Contracting Parties to the Convention. The Convention differentiates between the right of complaint for States on the one hand and that for individuals on the other.

1. The European Court of Human Rights: composition and structure

The number of judges of the European Court of Human Rights is equal to the number of High Contracting Parties. Article 21 of the Convention sets forth the criteria for office of the judges, dictating that they "shall be of high moral character and must either possess the qualifications required for appointment to high judicial office or be jurisconsults of recognised competence". They sit in their individual capacity and during their terms of office may not engage in any activity that is incompatible with their independence, impartiality or the demands of a full-time office. Judges are elected by the Parliamentary Assembly with respect to each High Contracting Party by a majority of votes cast from a list of three candidates submitted by that High Contracting Party. Judges serve for six-year terms and may be re-elected. The term of any judge expires when he or she reaches the age of seventy.

In the interests of efficiency, the Court is organised into Committees of three judges, Chambers of seven judges and a Grand Chamber of seventeen judges. Committees of three judges may, by a unanimous vote, declare inadmissible or strike out of their list of cases any individual application where such a decision can be taken without further examination. Chambers of seven judges decide on the admissibility and merits of cases not eliminated from the list by a Committee, as well as on the admissibility and merits of inter-State applications. If a Chamber considers that a case pending before it raises a serious question of interpretation of the Convention, or if there is a risk that its judgment in the case may be inconsistent with a previous judgment, a Chamber may relinquish jurisdiction in favour of the Grand Chamber, unless one of the parties to the case objects. A panel of five judges of the Grand Chamber may also consider requests from any party to a case that has been decided by a Chamber to review the case at issue and render its own judgment. Such a request must be received within three months of the date of the judgment of the Chamber. When deciding whether or not to review a case anew, the Grand Chamber considers whether the case raises "a serious question affecting the interpretation or application of the Convention or the protocols thereto, or a serious issue of general importance" (Article 43). The judge elected in respect of the State Party concerned sits on an ex officio basis in both the Chamber and Grand Chamber dealing with a case from his or her State Party.

2. The European Court of Human Rights: jurisdiction

The European Court of Human Rights exercises two types of jurisdiction. Under Article 47, the Committee of Ministers may request the Court to give an advisory opinion on any legal question concerning the interpretation of the Convention and the protocols thereto, as long as the opinion will not deal with any question relating to the content or scope of the rights guaranteed or with any question that the Court or Committee might have to consider in conjunction with proceedings instituted under the Convention.

The year 2002 saw the first time the Committee of Ministers requested an advisory opinion from the Court under Article 47 of the Convention. The request related to the co-existence of the Convention on Human Rights and Fundamental Freedoms of the Commonwealth of Independent States and the European Convention on Human Rights. On receipt of the request, the Court communicated it to the governments of all Contracting Parties, asking them to submit any written comments they might wish to make regarding the question of whether the request fell within the scope of the Court's advisory jurisdiction. Several Governments submitted comments in response. At the end of 2003, the proceedings were still pending.

By far the more important jurisdiction exercised by the Court is its contentious jurisdiction in inter-State and individual cases. On ratifying the European Convention on Human Rights, a state automatically accepts the jurisdiction of the European Court of Human Rights to review inter-State complaints under Article 33 and individual complaints under Article 34.

Inter-State complaints: Article 33

Article 33

> Any High Contracting Party may refer to the Court any alleged breach of the provisions of the Convention and the protocols thereto by another High Contracting Party.

Under this provision, a State may lodge a complaint about violations committed against persons who are not nationals of any of the Contracting States, and even about violations against nationals of the respondent state. In this way the right of inter-State complaint resembles an *actio popularis*.

Because state-to-state applications do not require that one state claim to be a "victim", the Court has broad competence *ratione personae* under Article 33. In instances where a state complains about the legislation or administrative practices of another Contracting Party, the complaining state need not even assert that there are specific victims of the alleged violations. In such a case, any alleged violation of the guaranteed rights is a sufficient cause for action. In the case of *Ireland v. the United Kingdom* (1978), the Court stated that in inter-State applications:

> [A] "breach" results from the mere existence of a law which introduces, directs or authorises measures incompatible with the rights and freedoms safeguarded....
>
> Nevertheless, the institutions established by the Convention may find a breach of this kind only if the law challenged pursuant to Article [33] is couched in terms sufficiently clear and precise to make the breach immediately apparent; otherwise, the decision of the Convention institutions must be arrived at by reference to the manner in which the respondent state interprets and applies *in concreto* the impugned text or texts.

The Court invoked this principle also in the case of *Cyprus v. Turkey* (2001), finding a violation of Article 6 of the Convention in the existence of a "legislative" practice of authorising the trial of civilians by military courts.

The right of individual petition: Article 34

Article 34

> The Court may receive applications from any person, non-governmental organisation or group of individuals claiming to be the victim of a violation by one of the High Contracting Parties of the rights set forth in the Convention or the protocols thereto. The High Contracting Parties undertake not to hinder in any way the effective exercise of this right.

The right of individual petition, which represents one of the most effective means of protecting human rights, is the essential element of the supervisory system established by the Convention. The European Convention on Human Rights protects the rights of individuals, that is natural or legal persons, not groups as such. In practical terms this means that only parties who are directly affected by a violation of one or more of the rights protected under the Convention may bring a claim in Strasbourg. The Convention does not provide for *actio popularis*. Even in "group" applications, each individual within the group must allege to be a victim. However, a legal person, such as a registered association, may file an application on behalf of its members in appropriate circumstances (see, for example, *Cha'are Shalom Ve Tsedek v. France* (2000) and *Metropolitan Church of Bessarabia and Others v. Moldova* (2001)).

In the absence of any State declaration to the contrary, the Court is competent to examine any matters arising since the State ratified the Convention itself, subject to the admissibility requirements for applications set forth under Article 35. In a number of cases, however, the Court has reviewed matters that originally arose prior to that time, primarily in connection with claims that the length of domestic legal proceedings had contravened the "reasonable time" requirement under Article 6, where the proceedings had not been completed when the State ratified the Convention. In such circumstances, the Court will normally take into consideration the state of the proceedings as of the date of ratification, not only the facts arising since that date.

In recent years, questions have arisen as to the scope of the State's obligation "not to hinder in any way the effective exercise" of the right to individual petition under Article 34. The Court has held that the essence of this provision is to ensure that applicants or potential applicants can communicate freely with the Court without being subjected to any form of pressure from the authorities to withdraw or modify their complaints (*Akdivar and Others v. Turkey* (1996)).

3. Conditions of admissibility: Article 35

Article 35

1. The Court may only deal with the matter after all domestic remedies have been exhausted, according to the generally recognised rules of international law, and within a period of six months from the date on which the final decision was taken.

2. The Court shall not deal with any application submitted under Article 34 that:

a. is anonymous; or

b. is substantially the same as a matter that has already been examined by the Court or has already been submitted to another procedure of international investigation or settlement and contains no relevant new information.

3. The Court shall declare inadmissible any individual application submitted under Article 34 which it considers incompatible with the provisions of the Convention or the protocols thereto, manifestly ill-founded, or an abuse of the right of application.

4. The Court shall reject any application which it considers inadmissible under this Article. It may do so at any stage of the proceedings.

Paragraphs 1 and 4 of Article 35 apply to both inter-State and individual applications, whereas paragraphs 2 and 3 apply only to individual applications.

Exhaustion of domestic remedies

All international human rights judicial or quasi-judicial bodies with competence to review individual complaints against a State apply the rule that an individual must exhaust all available domestic remedies prior to filing a formal complaint with the international supervisory body. This reflects a general principle of international law that is founded on the belief that a State must be afforded every possible opportunity to rectify any violation of its international obligations through its own domestic legal channels, prior to being subjected to international review and/or supervision (*Hentrich v. France* (1994)). It is only if State authorities fail to re-establish a violated right or to provide just satisfaction for its violation that the Court will entertain the matter.

The term, "exhaustion of domestic remedies", has been interpreted to require an applicant to exhaust all remedies provided for by domestic law. Where alternative remedies exist in the domestic legal system, however, an individual applicant is required to exhaust only one channel that might have proven effective in his or her case. The notion of "exhaustion" encompasses the obligation for an applicant to appeal to the highest domestic level that could afford him or her relief. However, an applicant is only required to exhaust those remedies open to him or her as a right, not a privilege. Therefore, he or she is not obliged to seek certain social services (Appl. No. 214/56) or to seek a pardon from the executive, a process considered to be an "extraordinary remedy" and therefore not an effective one (Appl. No. 8395/78). When considering whether an applicant has exhausted domestic remedies, both the substance of the case as pursued at the domestic level and the effectiveness of the remedies available through the domestic system will be considered. An applicant is not obliged to invoke the European Convention on Human Rights in the domestic courts, so long as he or she has invoked domestic legal provisions with an essentially similar content (*Cardot v. France* (1991) and *Ahmet Sadik v. Greece* (1996)). However, an applicant must invoke the Convention where it provides the only legal basis for a given claim (*Deweer v. Belgium* (1980)). An applicant must also pursue any domestic procedural means which might prevent a breach of the Convention (*Barberà, Messegué, and Jabardo v. Spain* (1988)).

It is for the respondent State to raise any objection that a given applicant has not exhausted domestic remedies (Appl. No. 9120/80), but it is also for the respondent State to meet the burden of proving the existence of available and sufficient domestic remedies (Appl. No. 9013/80). Respondent States also have the burden of proving that the existing remedies are effective. In the event that an action for damages exists in respect of a violation of a right, such a remedy must be practical and not just theoretical (*Navarra v. France* (1993)). Similarly, the recognition of the principle that an individual has a right to compensation for expropriated property is insufficient where the individual remains both dispossessed and uncompensated after an unlawful expropriation (*Guillemin v. France* (1997)). Available domestic remedies may be found to be ineffective on the grounds that established precedent in a given State's law are clearly against the applicant's chance of success (*Keegan v. Ireland* (1994)) or indeed where the subject matter of an applicant's case corresponds directly to a case already disposed of by the domestic authorities (Appl. Nos. 7367/76 and 7819/77). Appeals against expulsion or deportation orders that do not serve to suspend the proposed orders cannot be considered effective remedies, at least in respect of claims under Article 3 (prohibition of torture, inhuman or degrading treatment or punishment) (Appl. Nos. 10400/83 and 10564/83). Finally, should an applicant's legal counsel state unequivocally that a pursuit of a particular remedy would have no prospects of success, the applicant is usually absolved from the obligation to pursue the matter (Appl. No. 10000/82). However, if counsel only expresses doubts as to a successful outcome, an applicant must comply with the exhaustion requirement of Article 35(1) (Appl. No. 10789/84).

It is important to note that where an application has been declared inadmissible for non-exhaustion of domestic remedies, this is only a temporary obstacle; the Court may re-examine the same application if submitted once the applicant has exhausted available domestic remedies.

The six-month rule

Article 35(1) requires applicants to lodge their applications with the Court within six months from the date of the final domestic decision on the matter at issue. This provision, which constitutes a restriction on the right of petition, must be interpreted narrowly. A letter from an applicant will be considered as an "application" for the purposes of the six-month rule, where the purpose of the application in sufficiently clear (*Papageorgiou v. Greece* (1997)).

The date from which the six-month time-limit runs refers not only to the date on which a domestic decision was taken, but also to the date on which the applicant became aware of this decision and as a result was able to file an application with the Court. The requirement of a six-month "statute of limitations" can only reasonably apply in instances where there is a concrete and identifiable event. Thus, in cases where no appeal is available against a decision or act of a public authority, the time limit begins to run from the moment the final decision or act takes effect (Appl. Nos. 8206/78 and 8440/78). Where an application concerns the enforcement of a legal provision whose effect is to produce a violation that is continuous in time, there is no possible "starting point" from which the six-month time limit can run (Appl. No. 8317/78).

Additional conditions of admissibility for individual applications

Paragraphs 2 and 3 of Article 35

Articles 35(2) and (3) of the Convention set out conditions of admissibility applicable only to individual applications. Under these provisions, the Court cannot deal with any application that is anonymous, substantially the same as a matter which has already been examined by the Court, or has already been submitted to another procedure of international investigation or settlement. In either of the two latter circumstances, the Court can entertain an application if it contains relevant new information.

The condition provided for in paragraph 2(b) of Article 35 reflects the principle that the same matter should not be tried more than once: *res judicata*. The text of the Article lays down two conditions relating to the "substantial similarity" criterion: the first applies to applications already examined by the Court and the second to applications submitted to other international bodies. The problem raised in the latter case was not of great practical importance when the Convention was first implemented, but has become increasingly important because of the establishment of other international bodies dealing with human rights matters, such as the Human Rights Committee (International Covenant on Civil and Political Rights). The notion of "relevant new information" encompasses only facts that were not known at the time of the previous application or have occurred since the Court originally disposed of the matter.

Article 35(3) requires the Court to declare an application inadmissible if it is "incompatible with the provisions of the present Convention or the protocols thereto, manifestly ill-founded, or an abuse of the right of petition". The concept of incompatibility has been applied in instances when the subject matter of a given application is considered to have fallen outside the scope of the competence of the Convention organs.

The second term in Article 35(3), "manifestly ill-founded", has given rise to an abundance of case-law. This condition of admissibility prevents the Court from being obliged to examine an application on the merits if, on a preliminary examination, it does not appear to fall within the purview of the Convention. An application will be declared manifestly ill-founded at an early stage only if an examination of the application makes it impossible to envisage a violation of the Convention.

The third term of Article 35(3), "abuse of the right of petition", has not often been invoked in rejecting an application as inadmissible. The term has, however, been invoked where an applicant failed to respond to several requests in relation to the review of his or her application and where an applicant has, for example, made defamatory statements vis-à-vis the representatives of the respondent Government.

4. Proceedings on the merits

Once the Court declares an application admissible, Article 38 of the Convention comes into play. This Article provides for the following two courses of action.

Examination of a case

Paragraph 1(a) of Article 38 calls for the Court to pursue its examination of an admitted case together with the representatives of the parties. It also leaves it to the discretion of the Court to undertake any investigation that it deems necessary. Should it do so, the provision calls on the States concerned "to furnish all necessary facilities", an obligation that comprises such actions as making witnesses available, permitting access to detention facilities and so forth.

Friendly settlement proceedings

Paragraph 1(b) of Article 38 places the Court at the disposal of the parties, "with a view to securing a friendly settlement of the matter on the basis of respect for human rights as defined in the Convention and the protocols thereto". Friendly settlement proceedings are confidential (Article 38(2)).

Article 38(1)(b) describes the two aspects of friendly settlement proceedings. The first is mediation between the parties. The second, to ensure that any friendly settlement is made "on the basis of respect for human rights" is the principle governing such mediation. The Court's role in any settlement procedure is thus to guarantee the collective interest in respect for human rights – even in a specific case where the parties agree to settle a given matter between themselves. This function of the Court as impartial protector of human rights is particularly important where the consequences of a given violation go beyond the interest of the individual applicant who brought the case and where those consequences may require the State involved to adopt general measures to preclude future violations of the same right vis-à-vis other individuals. Many friendly settlements have been reached when the government of the respondent State has taken administrative or, in some cases, legislative measures to rectify a possible violation of the Convention. Others have been reached on the payment of an agreed sum of money to the applicant.

Should the Court effect a friendly settlement under Article 38(1)(b), it strikes the case out of its list in a decision that takes the form of a judgment. Once the judgment has become final, the Court forwards the judgment to the Committee of Ministers, whose role it is to supervise the execution of any undertakings which may have been attached to the settlement (Rule 43 of the Rules of the Court).

Unless there are "exceptional circumstances", all hearings before the Court are open to the public. In all circumstances, the judgment is announced publicly. The Court is not required to arrive at a unanimous decision and each judge is entitled to submit his or her own opinion which will be published with the majority opinion.

5. Other Court Procedures

Requests for interim measures: Rule 39 of the Rules of the Court

One important function of the European Court of Human Rights is not provided for in the Convention, but in Rule 39 of the Rules of Procedure of the Court. This rule allows a Chamber or its President to respond to the request of a party or other concerned person, or to act of its own motion, to "indicate to the parties any interim measure which it considers should be adopted in the interests of the parties or of the proper conduct of the proceedings before it". The main context in which the Court has exercised this function is where an applicant alleges that he or she will be subjected to a prohibited degree of ill-treatment if deported or extradited from a State Party. Should a State Party ignore a request under Rule 39, the Court will take that fact into consideration when determining whether there has been a violation of Article 3 (*Cruz Varas and Others v. Sweden* (1991)). It will also take it into consideration when determining whether there has been a breach of a State Party's obligation not to hinder in any way the effective exercise of the right of individual petition under Article 34 (*Mamatkulov and Abdurasulovic v. Turkey* (2004)).

Striking a case off the list: Article 37

The Court may sometimes strike a case off its list, a procedure that is governed by Article 37 of the Convention, which provides for this action when circumstances lead to the conclusion that the applicant does not intend to pursue his or her application, if the matter has been resolved, or if the Court establishes that it is no longer justified to continue the examination of the petition. The Court must retain any case on its list "if respect for human rights as defined in the Convention and the protocols thereto so requires".

Striking a case off the list is of particular importance where the withdrawal of the application or the applicant's inactivity is based on a prior agreement between him or her and the respondent State, without the participation or influence of the Court. Unlike in the "friendly settlement" procedure provided for in Article 38 of the Convention, because this informal form of settlement falls outside the Court's investigative procedures, it does not necessarily have to be concluded "on the basis of respect for human rights". However, the Court is competent to examine an application *ex officio,* even where an applicant has ceased to pursue or has declared the intention to withdraw his or her application.

Third-party interventions: Article 36

Article 36 governs third-party interventions before the Court. Paragraph 1 of this Article empowers any High Contracting Party one of whose nationals is an applicant both to submit written comments and to take part in hearings in the case.

Article 36(2) permits the President of the Court to invite any High Contracting Party that is not a party to the proceedings or any person concerned who is not the applicant also to submit such comments or to participate in such hearings. Any such discretionary third-party interventions must be "in the interest of the proper administration of justice".

Just satisfaction: Article 41

Article 41 of the European Convention on Human Rights provides that if a High Contracting Party is in breach of its obligations under the Convention, and if its domestic law does not provide for adequate reparation of that breach, then "the Court shall, if necessary, afford just satisfaction to the injured party". In many cases, the Court has found that the finding of a violation is in itself just satisfaction and in others that a token amount of money is sufficient. On the other hand, in some cases the Court awards substantial sums of money to successful applicants, including interest when the government unduly delays payment. On occasion, the Court has suggested that the most appropriate form of just satisfaction would be the return of unlawfully expropriated property to an applicant. Costs may also be awarded under Article 41.

The Court will usually address claims for just satisfaction under Article 41 in its judgment on the substantive aspects of the case. However, if the question is not then ready for decision, the Court may reserve it for a subsequent judgment.

6. Legal aid: Rules 91 to 96 and Rule 101

In the event that an applicant does not have sufficient means to meet the legal or other costs of pursuing his or her application to the Court, the president of a Chamber may grant the applicant free legal aid effective from the moment that the respondent Party submits its written observations on the admissibility of the application, or when the time limit for their submission has expired. In order to qualify for free legal aid from the Court, an applicant must complete a form of declaration of means that must be certified by the appropriate domestic authority or authorities. If the financial circumstances of the applicant change or the Court determines that it is no longer necessary, it may revoke or vary a grant of legal aid during the conduct of a case. Normally, however, the grant of legal aid is effective throughout the proceedings.

7. The Committee of Ministers of the Council of Europe

The Committee of Ministers of the Council of Europe is composed of the foreign ministers of all member States of the Council. Therefore, unlike the members of the European Court of Human Rights, the members of the Committee of Ministers serve in their capacities as governmental representatives, and not as individual human rights experts. The day-to-day work of the Committee of Ministers is normally carried out by their Deputies (the ambassadors of the member States). The power of the Committee of Ministers to request advisory opinions from the European Court of Human Rights is addressed above.

Article 46(1) provides that the High Contracting Parties undertake to abide by the final judgment of the Court in any case to which they are parties; and Article 46(2) provides that "[t]he final judgment of the Court shall be transmitted to the Committee of Ministers which shall supervise its execution". This supervision may take the form of monitoring legislative or administrative reforms instituted by States in response to a finding of a violation or, in the case of judgments for "just satisfaction" under Article 41, ensuring that the State has made its payment to the individual.

It is important to remember that the Committee of Ministers has no power to intervene directly in the supervision and execution of judgments by the offending State in a given case. Should a State choose to ignore or not to give full force to a judgment of the Court or a decision of the Committee of Ministers, there may often be little that the Committee of Ministers can do to persuade the State to respect the holding of the Strasbourg body. This being said, some of the most serious sanctions are not established by the European Convention on Human Rights itself, but are enshrined instead in the Statute of the Council of Europe. For example, Article 3 of the Statute provides that respect for human rights is a fundamental principle underlying participation in the Council; and Article 8 of the Statute empowers the Committee of Ministers to suspend or even to expel from the Council of Europe any member State guilty of serious human rights violations.

8. The Secretary General of the Council of Europe

The Secretary General acts as the depository for the European Convention on Human Rights, as is the case for all other conventions concluded by the Council of Europe. In some instances, the depository function is quite limited, for example, in regard to the Convention itself: under Article 59(4), the Secretary General only informs member States of the Council of Europe of the names of ratifying or acceding States.

The Secretary General is required to inform all High Contracting Parties of any State's denunciation of the European Convention on Human Rights under Article 58.

Under Article 15 of the Convention, any State derogating from its obligations under the Convention must keep the Secretary General fully informed of the measures taken and the reasons for so doing. The derogating State must also keep the Secretary General informed when it lifts the measures and returns the Convention to full operation. Throughout the period of derogation, the Secretary General has no express obligation to inform other High Contracting Parties of the derogation or its terms.

In addition to the Secretary General's function as a depository and, in some instances, a conduit for information to the High Contracting Parties to the Convention, the Secretary General performs other more direct functions in the supervision of the Convention. Article 52 empowers the Secretary General to request from any High Contracting Party "an explanation of the manner in which its internal law ensures the effective implementation of any of the provisions of this Convention". The Secretary General only occasionally requests such explanations; requests refer to a given issue and have to date been addressed to all High Contracting Parties, not to a particular State. It is important to note that Article 52 does not confer any power on the Secretary General to take any action in relation to information received from any High Contracting Party.

Concluding remarks

In spite of its deficiencies, this Guide has attempted to show how the European Convention on Human Rights, the world's strongest international legal instrument for the protection of the human rights of individuals, has evolved through its interpretation by the Convention institutions. The case-law from these bodies adds to the substance of the Convention, giving it form and life beyond the instrument itself. Their interpretations of such ideas as the rule of law and democratic society form the foundation of the European human rights system, and provide strong guidelines for central and east European countries who have recently become part of that system.

At the same time, a word of caution is in order. The European Convention on Human Rights is not a panacea for all human rights ills in Europe. Stemming as it does from the period immediately after the Second World War, it focuses exclusively on the individual and the protection of the individual's basic rights. As a result, at present, it lacks the capacity to address from a legal perspective many of the burning human rights issues of today, most notably economic and social rights. But in spite of the limitations of the European Convention on Human Rights, both politicians and lawyers should embrace the human rights tradition it embodies and work to improve upon its already admirable record. The admission into the Council of Europe and the accession to the European Convention on Human Rights of central and east European countries has provided a new impetus to these efforts, by forcing both the Council of Europe and its new and aspiring member States to scrutinise and evaluate their own performance and to recommit themselves to guaranteeing the high level of protection of human rights which forms the foundation of European moral and political life.

Appendices

Appendix 1:
The implementation machinery of the European Convention on Human Rights

Prior to 1 November 1998, two bodies exercised jurisdiction under the European Convention on Human Rights, the European Commission of Human Rights and the European Court of Human Rights. As of the afore-mentioned date, a revised European Convention on Human Rights provided for the exercise of such jurisdiction only by a single European Court of Human Rights. The following chart provides an overview of the procedural mechanisms of the European Court of Human Rights from 1 November 1998.

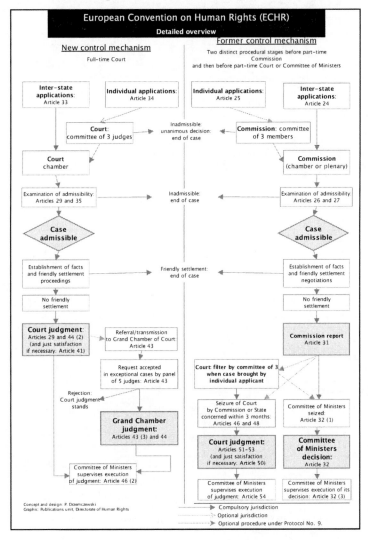

Appendix 2:
Chart of signatures and ratifications of the Convention and its Protocols

	European Convention on Human Rights	Protocol No. 1	Protocol No. 4	Protocol No. 6	Protocol No. 7	Protocol No. 12	Protocol No. 13	Protocol No. 14
Albania	02.10.96	02.10.96	02.10.96	21.09.00	02.10.96	26.11.04		
Andorra	22.01.96			22.01.96			26.03.03	
Armenia	26.04.02	26.04.02	26.04.02	29.09.03	26.04.02			
Austria	03.09.58	03.09.58	18.09.69	05.01.84	14.05.86		12.01.04	
Azerbaijan	15.04.02	15.04.02	15.04.02	15.04.02	15.04.02			
Belgium	14.06.55	14.06.55	21.09.70	10.12.98			23.06.03	
Bosnia and Herzegovina	12.07.02	12.07.02	12.07.02	12.07.02	12.07.02	29.07.03	29.07.03	
Bulgaria	07.09.92	07.09.92	04.11.00	29.09.99	04.11.00		13.02.03	
Croatia	05.11.97	05.11.97	05.11.97	05.11.97	05.11.97	03.02.03	03.02.03	
Cyprus	06.10.62	06.10.62	03.10.89	19.01.00	15.09.00	30.04.02	12.03.03	
Czech Republic	18.03.92	18.03.92	18.03.92	18.03.92	18.03.92		02.07.04	
Denmark	13.04.53	13.04.53	30.09.64	01.12.83	18.08.88		28.11.02	10.11.04
Estonia	16.04.96	16.04.96	16.04.96	17.04.98	16.04.96		25.02.04	
Finland	10.05.90	10.05.90	10.05.90	10.05.90	10.05.90		29.11.04	
France	03.05.74	03.05.74	03.05.74	17.02.86	17.02.86			
Georgia	20.05.99	07.06.02	13.04.00	13.04.00	13.04.00	15.06.01	22.05.03	10.11.04
Germany	05.12.52	13.02.57	01.06.68	05.07.89			11.10.04	
Greece	28.11.74	28.11.74			08.09.98	29.10.87		
Hungary	05.11.92	05.11.92	05.11.92	05.11.92	05.11.92		16.07.03	
Iceland	29.06.53	29.06.53	16.11.67	22.05.87	22.05.87		10.11.04	
Ireland	25.02.53	25.02.53	29.10.68	24.06.94	03.08.01		03.05.02	10.11.04
Italy	26.10.55	26.10.55	27.05.82	29.12.88	07.11.91			
Latvia	27.06.97	27.06.97	27.06.97	07.05.99	27.06.97			
Liechtenstein	08.09.82	14.11.95		15.11.90			05.12.02	
Lithuania	20.06.95	24.05.96	20.06.95	08.07.99	20.06.95		29.01.04	
Luxembourg	03.09.53	03.09.53	02.05.68	19.02.85	19.04.89			
Malta	23.01.67	23.01.67	05.06.02	26.03.91	15.01.03		03.05.02	04.10.04
Moldova	12.09.97	12.09.97	12.09.97	12.09.97	12.09.97			
Monaco								
Netherlands	31.08.54	31.08.54	23.06.82	25.04.86		28.07.04		
Norway	15.01.52	18.12.52	12.06.64	25.10.88	25.10.88			10.11.04
Poland	19.01.93	10.10.94	10.10.94	30.10.00	04.12.02			
Portugal	09.11.78	09.11.78	09.11.78	02.10.86			03.10.03	
Romania	20.06.94	20.06.94	20.06.94	20.06.94	20.06.94		07.04.03	
Russian Federation	05.05.98	05.05.98	05.05.98	05.05.98				
San Marino	22.03.89	22.03.89	22.03.89	22.03.89	22.03.89	25.04.03	25.04.03	
Serbia and Montenegro	03.03.04	03.03.04	03.03.04	03.03.04	03.03.04	03.03.04	03.03.04	
Slovakia	18.03.92	18.03.92	18.03.92	18.03.92	18.03.92			
Slovenia	28.06.94	28.06.94	28.06.94	28.06.94	28.06.94		04.12.03	
Spain	04.10.79	27.11.90		14.01.85				
Sweden	04.02.52	22.06.53	13.06.64	09.02.84	08.11.85		22.04.03	
Switzerland	28.11.74			13.10.87	24.02.88		03.05.02	
'the former Yugoslav Republic of Macedonia'	10.04.97	10.04.97	10.04.97	10.04.97	10.04.97	13.07.04	13.07.04	
Turkey	18.05.54	18.05.54		12.11.03				
Ukraine	11.09.97	11.09.97	11.09.97	04.04.00	11.09.97		11.03.03	
United Kingdom	08.03.51	03.11.52		20.05.99			10.10.03	

Updated: 17.03.05
Ratifications between 01.07.04 and 30.11.04 are highlighted
Full information on the state of signatures and ratifications of Council of Europe conventions can be found on the Treaty Office's Internet site: http://conventions.coe.int/

Sales agents for publications of the Council of Europe
Agents de vente des publications du Conseil de l'Europe

BELGIUM/BELGIQUE
La Librairie européenne SA
50, avenue A. Jonnart
B-1200 BRUXELLES 20
Tel.: (32) 2 734 0281
Fax: (32) 2 735 0860
E-mail: info@libeurop.be
http://www.libeurop.be

Jean de Lannoy
202, avenue du Roi
B-1190 BRUXELLES
Tel.: (32) 2 538 4308
Fax: (32) 2 538 0841
E-mail: jean.de.lannoy@euronet.be
http://www.jean-de-lannoy.be

CANADA
Renouf Publishing Company Limited
5369 Chemin Canotek Road
CDN-OTTAWA, Ontario, K1J 9J3
Tel.: (1) 613 745 2665
Fax: (1) 613 745 7660
E-mail: order.dept@renoufbooks.com
http://www.renoufbooks.com

CZECH REPUBLIC/
RÉPUBLIQUE TCHÈQUE
Suweco Cz Dovoz Tisku Praha
Ceskomoravska 21
CZ-18021 PRAHA 9
Tel.: (420) 2 660 35 364
Fax: (420) 2 683 30 42
E-mail: import@suweco.cz

DENMARK/DANEMARK
GAD Direct
Fiolstaede 31-33
DK-1171 COPENHAGEN K
Tel.: (45) 33 13 72 33
Fax: (45) 33 12 54 94
E-mail: info@gaddirect.dk

FINLAND/FINLANDE
Akateeminen Kirjakauppa
Keskuskatu 1, PO Box 218
FIN-00381 HELSINKI
Tel.: (358) 9 121 41
Fax: (358) 9 121 4450
E-mail: akatilaus@stockmann.fi
http://www.akatilaus.akateeminen.com

FRANCE
La Documentation française
(Diffusion/Vente France entière)
124, rue H. Barbusse
F-93308 AUBERVILLIERS Cedex
Tel.: (33) 01 40 15 70 00
Fax: (33) 01 40 15 68 00
E-mail:
commandes.vel@ladocfrancaise.gouv.fr
http://www.ladocfrancaise.gouv.fr

Librairie Kléber (Vente Strasbourg)
Palais de l'Europe
F-67075 STRASBOURG Cedex
Fax: (33) 03 88 52 91 21
E-mail: librairie.kleber@coe.int

GERMANY/ALLEMAGNE
AUSTRIA/AUTRICHE
UNO Verlag
August-Bebel-Allee 6
D-53175 BONN
Tel.: (49) 2 28 94 90 20
Fax: (49) 2 28 94 90 222
E-mail: bestellung@uno-verlag.de
http://www.uno-verlag.de

GREECE/GRÈCE
Librairie Kauffmann
28, rue Stadiou
GR-ATHINAI 10564
Tel.: (30) 1 32 22 160
Fax: (30) 1 32 30 320
E-mail: ord@otenet.gr

HUNGARY/HONGRIE
Euro Info Service
Hungexpo Europa Kozpont ter 1
H-1101 BUDAPEST
Tel.: (361) 264 8270
Fax: (361) 264 8271
E-mail: euroinfo@euroinfo.hu
http://www.euroinfo.hu

ITALY/ITALIE
Libreria Commissionaria Sansoni
Via Duca di Calabria 1/1, CP 552
I-50125 FIRENZE
Tel.: (39) 556 4831
Fax: (39) 556 41257
E-mail: licosa@licosa.com
http://www.licosa.com

NETHERLANDS/PAYS-BAS
De Lindeboom Internationale
Publikaties
PO Box 202, MA de Ruyterstraat 20 A
NL-7480 AE HAAKSBERGEN
Tel.: (31) 53 574 0004
Fax: (31) 53 572 9296
E-mail: books@delindeboom.com
http://home-1-worldonline.nl/~lin-deboo/

NORWAY/NORVÈGE
Akademika, A/S Universitetsbokhandel
PO Box 84, Blindern
N-0314 OSLO
Tel.: (47) 22 85 30 30
Fax: (47) 23 12 24 20

POLAND/POLOGNE
Głowna Księgarnia Naukowa
im. B. Prusa
Krakowskie Przedmiescie 7
PL-00-068 WARSZAWA
Tel.: (48) 29 22 66
Fax: (48) 22 26 64 49
E-mail: inter@internews.com.pl
http://www.internews.com.pl

PORTUGAL
Livraria Portugal
Rua do Carmo, 70
P-1200 LISBOA
Tel.: (351) 13 47 49 82
Fax: (351) 13 47 02 64
E-mail: liv.portugal@mail.telepac.pt

SPAIN/ESPAGNE
Mundi-Prensa Libros SA
Castelló 37
E-28001 MADRID
Tel.: (34) 914 36 37 00
Fax: (34) 915 75 39 98
E-mail: libreria@mundiprensa.es
http://www.mundiprensa.com

SWITZERLAND/SUISSE
Adeco – Van Diermen
Chemin du Lacuez 41
CH-1807 BLONAY
Tel.: (41) 21 943 26 73
Fax: (41) 21 943 36 05
E-mail: info@adeco.org

UNITED KINGDOM/ROYAUME-UNI
TSO (formerly HMSO)
51 Nine Elms Lane
GB-LONDON SW8 5DR
Tel.: (44) 207 873 8372
Fax: (44) 207 873 8200
E-mail: customer.services@theso.co.uk
http://www.the-stationery-office.co.uk
http://www.itsofficial.net

UNITED STATES and CANADA/
ÉTATS-UNIS et CANADA
Manhattan Publishing Company
2036 Albany Post Road
CROTON-ON-HUDSON,
NY 10520, USA
Tel.: (1) 914 271 5194
Fax: (1) 914 271 5856
E-mail: Info@manhattanpublishing.com
http://www.manhattanpublishing.com

Council of Europe Publishing/Editions du Conseil de l'Europe
F-67075 Strasbourg Cedex
Tel.: (33) 03 88 41 25 81 – Fax: (33) 03 88 41 39 10 – E-mail: publishing@coe.int – Website: http://book.coe.int